Every best wish
Michael Mannion C.P.
September 1979

To
Our Lady of Czestochowa
and
the Martyrs of Poland

Michael O'Carroll, C.S.Sp.

Poland and John Paul II

Veritas Publications Dublin

First published 1979 by
Veritas Publications,
7-8 Lower Abbey Street,
Dublin 1.

Cover design by Richard Whyte

Cover photograph
Portrait study by Karsh of Ottawa,
Copyright Camera Press, London.

ISBN 0 905092 89 9
Cat. No. 3392

Origination by Joe Healy Typesetting, Dublin 2.
Printed and bound in the Republic of Ireland by
Genprint Limited, Dublin 9.

Contents

Introduction   vii
1 The country   1
2 The Nazis   9
3 The Stalinists   28
4 Bishop   40
5 Church and State   52
6 Cardinal   63
7 Pope   79
8 Homecoming   92
   Select Bibliography   110

Introduction

It will take some time for the Catholic faithful and those who respect the papacy to grasp what happened on the evening of 16 October 1978, in Vatican City. For the second time within two months the media reporters were confounded. When Cardinal Felici paused after the word "Carolum" there was mostly blank surprise. "Who is he?" Some remembered that Cardinal Confalonierei bore the Christian name. "But surely not him at the age of eighty-five?" Cardinal Wojtyla's name had not been unknown but it had remained peripheral.

"And now the most eminent Cardinals have called a new Bishop of Rome. They have called him from a distant country, distant but always close in the communion of faith and Christian tradition." This was not only the first non-Italian Pope since Adrian VI was elected in 1522, but also the first Pole and the first representative of the Slav peoples.

Karol Wojtyla was the first man, in seventeen centuries, to mount the throne of Peter from a community of martyrs. We are not talking metaphors. The martyrology of Poland contains 3,000 names of priests and religious who were interned or driven from their domiciles. The death-roll, through ill-treatment or murder, includes six bishops, 2,030 priests, 127 seminarists, 173 male religious, 243 nuns. These were the Pope's contemporaries, many of them very close to him. When he was working in a Krakow quarry and in the Solway company's chemical factory the Franciscan martyr, Blessed Maximilian Kolbe, was already doomed; he would meet his death in Auschwitz concentration camp near Karol Wojtyla's home town. There too, died Edith Stein, the convert Jewess, formerly Husserl's pupil, now a Carmelite sister, Teresa

Benedicta of the Cross; one day, it is hoped, she too will be beatified.

Never since the *Te Deum* has been sung in St Peter's at the election of a Pope has one verse had such poignant relevance: *Te martyrum candidatus laudat exercitus.* If the communion of saints has any meaning, countless bright spirits must have surrounded this man at this moment, the martyrs of Poland rejoicing with the universal Church.

For a while the Iron Curtain was forgotten. The Church of Silence gave a voice to the universal Church. The world, especially the world of believers, inevitably became conscious of the country from which the Pope came. His election was a judgement not only on an individual but on a people. In choosing Karol Wojtyla the cardinals, in a sense, chose Poland. I have tried in this book to relate the career of the man to the history of the country. The story is a commentary on these words spoken by the Pope:

> And here we have a significant thing, difficult to understand on the human plane. Just in these last decades the Church in Poland has acquired a special significance in the context of the universal Church and of Christendom. The Church in Poland has become an object of great interest owing to a specific system of relations, a system which has so much importance in the efforts that modern man, various peoples and states, are making in the social, economic and cultural fields. The Church in Poland has acquired a new voice, it has become the Church of a special witness to which the whole world looks. In this Church, our people, today's generation, lives and expresses itself.

> *Unless this fact is accepted* [my italics], it is not possible to understand why a "Polish Pope" is speaking to you today. It is difficult to understand how a conclave which, on 26 August (the feast of Our Lady of Czestochowa) had made a magnificent gift to the Church in the person of the Holy Father John Paul I, subsequently, after his unforgettable death which took place after just thirty-three days pontificate, called a Polish cardinal to St Peter's Chair. It is difficult to understand how this choice did not meet opposition but understanding and even benevolent acceptance.

As well as the 34 million Poles in the homeland there are ten million people throughout the world who claim direct Polish descent: six million in the United States, which has a Cardinal, ten bishops, 1,700 priests and 7,000 nuns from this strong minority; over 700,000 in France; 100,000 in Great Britain; far-flung communities like the Poles who greeted John Paul II in Mexico. There is a world Polish presence which retains links with the mother country and enriches with striking talent the land of adoption: witness Felix Topolski, whose remarkable drawings caught the historic moment in St Peter's Square on 22 October 1978 when his fellow Pole was enthroned.

Inside the country the socio-religious position is bizarre, the political situation complex. The regime is maintained by Russia which means the Red Army. But the government has problems when its Polish identity asserts itself. Can it be sure of the western frontier without Russia? If it were to push independence too far would Poland escape what happened to Hungary in 1956 and to Czechoslovakia in 1968?

It is bizarre that a predominantly Catholic people is at the mercy of a small group which, with control of power and of resources, can harass those it dislikes. Symbolic of this vexed situation is the presence in the cabinet of a Minister for Religious Affairs who is a convinced Marxist atheist; or again, the refusal, up to the enthronement Mass of John Paul II, to allow any Catholic service on radio or television; or again, the restrictions on the Catholic press and the operation of censorship.

Apart from drawing on an abundant literature I have been helped by a number of people whom I wish to thank: Jan Zaborowski and those of the Christian Social Association who, with him, produce the *Information Bulletin,* in the files of which I got much information; Fr Eugene Banasiuk of Czestochowa Monastery who was my guide in Krakow and Nowa Huta; and Fr Henryk Fros, S.J. of Krakow, now with the Bollandistes in Brussels, who let me see the MS of his article on Cardinal Wojtyla's book on the Council.

I wish, also, to thank Fr Pearse Moloney, C.S.Sp., Secretary General, for sending me with no loss of time the copies of *L'Osservatore Romano,* 3-11 June, on which chapter 8 is based and Fr Matthew Farrelly, C.S.Sp., Representative to the Holy See, for a similar service in regard to the early chapters.

1 The country

This year is the bicentennial of the day when the hunger
for freedom ripened in American society and revealed itself in liberation and the Declaration of Independence of
the United States. Tadeusz Kosciuszko and Kasimierz
Pulaski, my fellow-countrymen, took part in this fight
for independence. The heroes of the Polish nation became
the heroes of American independence. All this took place
at a time when the Polish kingdom, a large state consist-
ing of three nations, the Poles, the Lithuanians and
Ruthenians, was beginning to lose its independence,
gradually becoming the prey of its rapacious neighbours,
Russia, Germany and Austria. At the time that the United
States were gaining independence we were losing it, lost
it in effect for more than a hundred years.

Many heroic efforts and sacrifices, similar to those of
Kosciuszko and Pulaski, have been called for, that the
nation's freedom should flower again, be established before the world and in time be expressed by the independence of our country. I wish to confess here before the
Eucharistic Jesus, that during the struggles for freedom
in former centuries and in our own, He was our inspiration and only hope. The faith in His resurrection from
the dead after His Passion and death has never left us
and, in spite of distress and persecution, has unfailingly
given us the will to live and the desire for freedom.

These words spoken by Cardinal Wojtyla on 3 August 1976,
at the International Eucharistic Congress in Philadelphia,
reveal the special Polish identity, the sense of history so
characteristic of Poles, the invincible spirit of a whole people
sharing closely a distinctive outlook: an outlook composed
of nationalism and the faith. The origins of the phenomenon
are in 966 when a strong ruler, Prince Mieskzo, appears at
the head of an organised state and, having married a Czech

Christian princess, Dobrova, himself asks for baptism. So quickly did Christianity grow from his example and support that a hierarchy was well begun by the year 1000.

To insure against grasping neighbours, Prince Mieszko placed his lands under the special protection of the Pope: he was a voluntary vassal. So, in his own way, he played Constantine as well as Clovis. The faith and the national ethos were thus interwoven. The fruits of the alliance are something for the Poles to look back on with pride. The great religious orders were implanted through the country. Saints arose to cast a spell not only in their own time but right down to ours, Adalbert, Hedwiga, Jan Kenty, Stanislaus of Krakow — the Polish Thomas a Becket, martyred nine hundred years ago, a century before Becket, because he, too, dared to say to an overweening ruler: "Thus far and no further."

The Poles did not take part in the Crusades. They had their high Middle Ages with a flowering of culture which still charms the visitor to the old medieval market in Warsaw or to the beautiful city of Krakow. Krakow has the oldest university in eastern Europe, justly renowned. In the Mary Church, the Mariaski, the carved lindenwood altar by Wit Stwosz is a thing of entrancing beauty. You will be told, rightly, that he was as Polish as El Greco was Spanish!

The Reformation, with its attendant wars of religion, came upon that splendour. In Poland, Sweden was the Protestant enemy. The Swedes overran the country in the seventeenth century and trusting their luck or ignoring the imponderables moved up to the gates of a Paulite monastery fortress on a hill above Czestochowa. This was their undoing. The prior of the day, Augustine Kordecki, raised a scratch force, imbued it with spirit and sent the invader reeling back in dismay. Polish soil remained Catholic.

In the next century, Poland was sufficiently Catholic to save Europe from the Turks. The crucial episode had everything that is Polish, romance, daring, gallantry and the faith. John Sobieski, the man Chesterton forgot when he wrote about the "last knight of Europe", arrived at the gates of

Vienna in 1683, just as the beleagured citizens were in despair. The night before he moved in, they saw his signal fires on the heights of Kahlenberg and the next day the invader felt his power.

The kings that followed were not of the same stuff. The monarchy which had served Poland well began to decay; it was sapped by an elective system. Then in the eighteenth century came the carve-up of the national territory, carried out in three phases until the name of Poland vanished from the map. Frederick the Great, one of the greedy neighbours, made a cynical gibe at the country's religion: "Let us partake of the eucharistic body of Poland." Another, Maria Theresa of Austria, wept for the Poles but took her share. Catherine of Russia was not given to tears in such circumstances. The desolation was lit by the bright name of Kosciusko, whom Cardinal Wojtyla recalled in Philadelphia. He was a legend in his country's story, a hero too of the American war of Independence, Washington's friend.

Karol Wojtyla was born in the moment of his country's resurrection. The era of the partitions ended with the Treaty of Versailles which concluded the First World War. In the lands ruled by Prussia and Russia, that era had been a time of intermittent persecution. Nonetheless, across all the partition lines, the consciousness of separate national identity had never waned.

The old enemy in the east, now in the hands of the Bolsheviks, sent a military force to the Vistula, hoping that the rest of the Marxist apparatus would follow in due course. The hero of the final struggle, Joseph Pilsudski, met them on the river and, with some French help, routed them. Bolshevism was momentarily contained. The national leader, Pilsudski, a member of the Second Socialist International, lies near the kings of Poland in the chapel of the Wawel above Krakow. He was not the last to prove that Polish blood is thicker than socialist water.

A Vatican diplomat called Ratti was in Warsaw from the first days of the new state. He advised on matters such as the foundation of the Catholic University of Lublin. He became an adopted Pole from the moment of peril, being the only member of the diplomatic corps who did not leave the city during the Battle of the Vistula. He was named Nuncio when government was fully established. In 1925, as Pius XI, he signed a Concordat with the government and, in that year, by the Apostolic Brief, *Vixdum Poloniae Unitas,* he satisfactorily established a diocesan system over the reunited motherland. He died before the two tyrannies, German and Russian, joined hands again to divide Poland and wreak horror on its people.

Any doubt on Polish Catholicism, had there been such, must have dissolved as those interested watched the bearing of these Catholics through the prolonged ordeal. They had been well prepared. The years between 1919 and 1939 had seen progress in many sectors of Church life. Religious orders and congregations flourished. Priestly vocations were numerous. Theology was well taught in the seminaries and in the Catholic university faculties such as those of Kracow and Lublin. Polish names appeared with distinction in responsible posts within the whole Church. The Ledochowski family, for example, had already given a cardinal capable of resisting Bismark and now could point to his nephew, Wladimir, Master General of the Jesuits, and his niece in the same family, Blessed Maria Teresa Ledochowska, foundress of the Society of St Peter Claver. The tradition of the priest-scientist deriving from Copernicus came alive in Bohenski, a Dominican, one of the originators of mathematical logic. Publications, scholarly and popular, were abundant in every area of Catholic thought.

The Polish church has always maintained strong links with the Papacy through its hierarchy, and the bishops themselves have had a close sense of corporate unity about the primate. This office was held on the eve of World War II by Augustus Cardinal Hlond, supported in Church government by twenty-one bishops.

An exceptional Christian morale had matured within a church so well structured. The Poles would draw on that spirit when the structure was torn, defaced and battered. A unique element in this Catholicism is the attitude to the Blessed Virgin Mary. Polish Catholicism is a constant collective affirmation of the Mother of God.

The symbols of this spiritual impulse are over 300 Marian sanctuaries cherished through the land. One such shrine in Piekary, Upper Silesia, the heart of working-class Poland, has drawn attention recently. "How would the workers respond to the ancient piety?" "In hundreds of thousands". In 1978 for the patronal feast in May, Piekary saw the largest pilgrimage in its history, 300,000 strong. The preacher was the future John Paul II.

But the hearthstone of the Catholic nation will for ever remain Czestochowa, Jasna Gora, the bright mountain above the city where the Paulite monastery houses an illustrious icon. Let John Paul II have a word to enlighten us. In his first papal letter to his fellow-countrymen, he wrote:

> Venerable and beloved Cardinal Primate, allow me to tell you just what I think. The Polish Pope who today full of fear of God, but also of trust, is beginning a new pontificate, would not be on Peter's chair were it not for your faith which did not retreat before prison and suffering, were it not for your heroic hope, your unlimited trust in the Mother of the Church, were it not for Jasna Gora and the whole period of the history of the Church in our country together with your ministry as Bishop and Primate.

Here the Pope is echoing the words spoken by the primate before the fathers of Vatican II. If Poland survived the shocks of the sixteenth century and the twentieth, this was due to be Blessed Virgin Mary; Our Lady of Czestochowa, he would also have said.

In this secularised age, western theologians should restrain their scepticism in face of such assertions. Poland stands on the frontier between Latin and Orthodox Christianity. Addressing a meeting of theologians, Cardinal Wojtyla once said that this fact could give them a special role in understanding and interpreting Orthodox traditions.

The icon, in this eastern world, has a place of importance, a meaning very much superior to that accorded to holy images in the west. It is a symbol of divine things. The icon is not a product of arbitrary individual choice but is made in a spirit of self-discipline, in submission to church traditions. Once enshrined, it speaks of God; is in a way a vehicle of his revelation. Hence modern Orthodox theologians, foremost among them the spiritual giant Sergius Bulgakov, developed their theology, especially of the Blessed Virgin, from overt contemplation of icons. This is the world we enter when we watch the icon of Czestochowa on pilgrimage through the cities and countryside of Poland: a world of divine light and power. Among the international roll-call in the visitors' book at Czestochowa, a quite illegible scrawl is said to be the signature of Adolf Hitler.

The year 1982 will be the six hundredth anniversary of the arrival of the icon of Our Lady in Czestochowa. To take only the lifetime of Karol Wojtyla as a period in which to study its effects would occupy much space. In 1920, the year of his birth, the bishops of Poland consecrated their country to the Sacred Heart of Jesus before the icon of the Mother. They there renewed the proclamation of Our Lady as Queen of Poland, which had been made by King John Casimir in Lwow cathedral in 1656, the year after the victory over the Swedes at Czestochowa. On 8 September 1946, the year of Karol Wojtyla's priestly ordination, Augustus Cardinal Hlond and the whole hierarchy dedicated the nation to the Immaculate Heart of Mary, following the example of Pius XII who had so consecrated the world on 31 October 1942. The important events of the year 1956, the novena of preparation for the Millennium in 1966, and the climax of Church-State tension in that year, were all related to Jasna Gora.

Such traditions make Polish Catholicism distinctive. It is also homogeneous through the nation and its overseas expansion. There is, however, one dissident body, which seeks, as its name "The Polish National Catholic Church" implies, to retain the Catholic faith and Church organisation while emphasising the national aspect. The Polish National Catholic

Church exists mostly in the United States where it origi-
nated, but it has supporting membership in the motherland.

When towards the end of the last century Polish emigrants
began to arrive in the United States they found themselves
increasingly at odds with the established church administration. Leadership was predominantly Irish and German and
tenure of church property was on a system the Poles disliked;
the rules had been laid down by the Council of Baltimore.
The newcomers wanted also, understandably, to hear sermons in their own language.

Dissatisfaction took an organised form in 1895 when
Anton Koslowski, at one time assistant priest in St Jad-
wiga's parish, Chicago, set up an independent congregation
in the church of All Saints in the same diocese. Two years
later he was consecrated bishop by an Old Catholic bishop
in Switzerland. From then until his death ten years later he
set up twenty-three parishes from New Jersey to Manitoba,
giving them the name, "The Polish Old Catholic Church".
He consecrated no bishop. Another bishop had, however,
appeared on the scene during his lifetime. When in 1895,
the Poles in the parish of St Adalbert, Buffalo, quarrelled
with their bishop over ecclesiastical property, they organised
a rival parish which they called Our Lady of the Rosary.
Their parish priest, Stanislaus Kaminski, had himself consecrated bishop by an itinerant prelate whose own affilia-
tion was constantly in flux but whose orders seem to have
been valid, Joseph René Vilatte. Kaminski claimed no writ
beyond his own parish.

Bishop Francis Hodur certainly did so. Again the starting
point was church property. The Polish parishioners of the
Sacred Heart church in Scranton refused to cede the legal title
of the building to the bishop. On advice from Hodur, who
had been assistant priest in the parish, they built a new
church, refused to hand it over to the bishop and accepted
Hodur as their parish priest. After a fruitless visit to Rome
and despite excommunication he established an independent
congregation, naming the parish for St Stanislaus. A synod
was held in 1904 and the parish priest was elected bishop.

The Old Catholics would not consecrate him until Koslow-ski died. In 1907 the ceremony took place in Utrecht.

The movement now had a dynamic leader who extended and organised it until he died, blind and paralysed, at the age of eighty-six in 1953. Most of the dissident Polish Catholics joined and eventually there were members from nine states. Numbers increased between 1926 and 1936 from 61,000 to 186,000. Four bishops were consecrated by Hodur, who took the title Prime Bishop, and a seminary was founded in Scranton.

The synod meets every four years bringing together bishops, parish priests and lay delegates. It is influenced by the Prime Bisop who heads the central diocese, consecrates other bishops, controls the seminary and church publications, examines candidates for the priesthood, and submits a list of priests eligible for choice as bishops by the synod.

In general, Catholic doctrine and practice are maintained with some notable exceptions. Polish was used in the Liturgy from 1900. Priests were allowed to marry though not many did so out of respect for the lay members. Baptism and Confirmation were made into one Sacrament and preaching, reading and hearing the Word of God became the seventh. Hodur was guilty of doctrinal wooliness; he does not seem to have believed in original sin or hell, and taught that "before God and before America all beliefs, all sects, are equal". He instituted feasts of a nationalist kind.

In 1921 the fourth synod officially authorised a mission to Poland and eventually there was a bishop, Joseph Padewski, consecrated by Hodur, with 56 parishes, a seminary in Krakow and some 50,000 faithful. The church suffered during the war and there were but 70 priest survivors. The Stalinists blew hot and cold on the National Church. In 1951 all contact with the United States was severed. Padewski was imprisoned and died in a Warsaw prison on 10 May 1951.

The future of a Polish dissident church in the pontificate of a Polish Pope will be an intriguing phenomenon to watch.

2   The Nazis

My beloved brothers and sisters, allow me to thank you
for all the years of my life, years of study, of priesthood,
of episcopate. How could I know that all these years
would prepare me for the call which I received from Christ
on 16 October in the Sistine chapel? However, in the perspective of what took place on that day I must turn my
thoughts to all those who, without knowing it, prepared
me for this call; my beloved parents whose lives ended so
long ago; my parish, Wadowice, dedicated to the Presentation of the Blessed Virgin in the Temple. the primary
and secondary schools; the Jagiellonian University, the
theology faculty; the ecclesiastical seminary. What should
I say of my predecessor in the see of St Stanislaus, Cardinal Adam Stefan Sapieha and of the great exile Archbishop
Eugeniusz Baziak, of the bishops, of the priests and of so
many fervent pastors, profound and excellent teachers,
of the exemplary men and women religious; of the many
lay people from different walks of life that I have met;
of my companions at school, at the university and in the
seminary; of the Solway workers, of the intellectuals,
writers, artists, people from different professions . . .

These words are the groundplan of John Paul II's bio-
graphy traced by the subject. Hagiography will heavily em-
broider it. Let us try to keep to the facts, which are not
dull. Karol Wojtyla is a southern Pole. His family came from
the mountain district along the Czechoslovak border;
some had settled in the town of Wadowice, in Upper Silesia,
about thirty miles southwest of Krakow, within twenty
miles of Auschwitz, a spot marked with infamy in the
Pope's lifetime. In Wadowice, the future Pope was born on
18 May 1920 to Karol Wojtyla and Emilia, née Kaczorowska.
The town was a country market centre, with a popula-

tion of some 9,000 inhabitants. The boy's father was an army sergeant, serving on the regional draft board; the mother had been a teacher. They lived with their first child, a boy Edward, fifteen years older than Karol, in a three-room apartment on the first floor of 7 Koscielna Street, in the vicinity of the parish church. The house which has been much photographed recently has been renovated since those days; it was fairly poor with few modern facilities. The mother did some sewing to supplement the family income. Both boys received a university education; the elder brother, a doctor, died during a scarlatina epidemic.

Karol Lolus, "Lolek" to his friends, was not baptised until 20 June, over a month after his birth. In due course he went to the town primary school. Since he is still under sixty, reporters and others have been able to talk to former class-mates. Has the amazing subsequent career thrown back over the early days a glow of artificial light and triumph? The anti-triumphalists have some obstacles, some certain facts, when we move a stage further in the story. In 1931 Karol Wojtyla entered the town secondary school, the Gymnasium. He was already touched by adversity, for his mother had died two years earlier; she died in childbirth, delivered of a baby girl who was stillborn. Those who have taught for years and known children thus deprived of a mother's presence, will see something others may miss in those photographs which have been collected and published of the Pope's childhood: that eager little face, prematurely serious, the wide open eyes, that indefinable sense of bareness.

The father, it is said, was strict, as army men can be in the home. He was a great reader, interested in history and, in one photograph, he has the intense look of a student rather than that of a military man. He certainly encouraged religious practice for Karol was an altar-boy, sang in the church choir, and went to Mass daily.

Two things are remembered about his secondary schooling. In his last year, 1939, Archbishop Adam Stefan Sapieha of Krakow came on a visit to Wadowice and its secondary school. Schools were not then a bone of contention between Church and State and Fr Edward Zacher, teacher of religious knowledge, was a member of the teaching staff. The address of welcome to the Archbishop was read by Karol Wojtyla. Sapieha, a prince by birth, but essentially a priest of God, asked Fr Zacher did this boy, who had impressed him, have any idea of the priesthood. The answer was negative.

The report sheet on the boy's final year at the school would have also impressed Sapieha. It shows that for conduct and six subjects — religious knowledge, Polish, Latin, Greek, German, mathematics — he won a "very good" (apparently the highest given) and for three subjects — physics, chemistry, history — he got "good". A former classmate thought that he never got less than "very good", an indication of his scholastic reputation. There is a story current that as a result of an accident in later years, after completion of his secondary studies, he was concussed and came back to full health with a curious bonus, an improved memory. One would want scientific evidence, since his memory was not, to judge from results, exactly mediocre. Fr Zacher, who taught him for six years, now says that he was the nearest thing to a schoolboy genius he ever met. Another teacher, Helena Szczepanska, says that Karol was the best in the school in Greek and Latin: "He sometimes embarrassed us, he seemed to know more than we did."

His outdoor interests were to remain with him into later years, swimming, walking, canoeing, skiing on the Tatras which are not very far from his home town. "Was he an outstanding player on the football team?" Doctor Wlodzimierz Pietrowski, a former team-mate, describes him thus: "He was not all that strong but he was a good player; he trained persistently to develop his muscles. He was not a joker, but his mind was like quicksilver. He was always deep in thought."

In 1931, when Karol completed his secondary studies, the Wojtyla family moved from Wadowice to Krakow. Except for two years in Rome after ordination the future

Pope spent the next forty years of his life in the ancient royal city of Poland, a city with physical beauty as its birthright and culture its natural ornament. Well did Cardinal Wojtyla, in 1975, ask the faithful of his diocese to offer prayers of thanksgiving to almighty God that such "priceless treasures" had been preserved. The face of Warsaw is Poland's face of power, of conflict on any scale when freedom is the prize, of victory at any price save honour. Krakow has a face of beauty, subtle, persuasive, patient and reflective. One of its glories is the Jagiellonian University, an institution prominent in the life of Karol Wojtyla. He went there on the completion of his secondary studies, returned later to supplement the clandestine theological course he had followed in the war years and, after another interval, to do post-graduate research, acting also as chaplain to the students. As bishop and cardinal he could maintain continuous contacts with professors and students, as his residence on Franciszkanska Street was beside the university campus.

There was no indication of such a future career in the first years Karol Wojtyla spent at Krakow University. He enrolled as a student of Polish language and literature, and philosophy. For a career his thoughts turned principally to the stage. He joined Studio Dramatyczne 1939, a student group which put on plays of Polish historical interest and some modern works. He studied for a diploma in drama. His performance in one play, "Moonlight Cavalier", by Marian Nijinski, is enthusiastically recalled by his fellow actors and actresses. The play was a hit, was well publicised and reviewed and is still referred to in histories of the Krakow theatre.

In his choice of companions and recreation Wojtyla's emphasis was very much on culture. He met with friends for verse readings, their own compositions or poetry published by authors whom they liked. His own choice was often the work of Emil Zegadlowicz, like himself a native of Wadowice. One of these ardent young people, Mieczyslaw Kotlarczyk, was to reach fame in the Polish theatre. A book dealing with his attainments as an actor entitled *The art of the living word,* carries a preface by his lifelong friend, by this time Archbishop of Krakow.

In September 1939, the world crashed about the two young friends. The ancient enemies of Poland had made another evil pact. Of the two tyrannies which then joined hands, Russian and German, the Nazi record is the blackest. The Poles did not provoke Hitler's paranoiac temper as did the Jews. They stung him, nonetheless, to a sustained icy fury. They refused to surrender. Alone of all his victims they gave him no quisling: their defiance was total, their honour resplendent.

Everyone who lived through the war years in Poland was indelibly marked, brought to a special maturity, by the terrible reality of the time. This was the catechesis of calamity. Wojtyla felt it at once. The University of Krakow was closed. On 6 November 1939, the entire teaching staff was assembled and, to their surprise and horror, taken off to concentration camps. Many of these teachers were world-famous scholars. Seventeen of them died in detention; the others, as a result of world protest and pressure, were eventually released.

From this episode the young man's mind would turn, in the years ahead, to a panorama of widespread torment. On 18 November 1965, with his fellow Polish bishops, he would sign a letter to the German hierarchy, which, while offering forgiveness and urging reconciliation, recalled the evils of the war:

> After a short independence lasting about twenty years (1918–1939) Poland, through no fault of her own, felt crashing upon her what has euphemistically been called the second world war, which by us was considered total annihilation. Our poor country sank into a dark and sinister night such as in generations we had never known. This night all of us called "the time of the German occupation" and thus it will remain in the history of Poland. We were reduced to helplessness. Our country was covered with concentration camps, in which chimneys from the crematoria smoked day and night. More than six million Polish citizens, in majority Jewish,

paid for the occupation with their lives. The Polish intelligentsia was simply swept away; 2,000 priests and
five bishops (one quarter of the existing hierarchy) went
into concentration camps. Hundreds of priests and tens
of thousands of civilians were the victims of summary
execution in the first days of the war (278 priests in the
diocese of Kulm alone). The diocese of Wloclawek lost
48 per cent of its priests during the war, Kulm 47 per
cent. Many others were deported. All secondary and higher schools were closed. Seminaries were suppressed. Every
German uniform, not only that of the SS, became for
every Pole an object of hatred. There is no Polish family
which has not war victims among its members. We do not
wish to give every detail so as not to open wounds which
are not yet healed, but if we recall the terrible night
through which Poland passed it is solely that our present
mentality should be understood . . ."

The Nazi programme was part of Karol Wojtyla's curri-
culum vitae. Even preaching to the papal household in
1976 he recalled the concentration camps. During the
war he was not in Warsaw, which has memories of the Pawiak
prison, where his hero Maximilian Kolbe began his martyrdom, of Gestapo interrogation cells, of the destruction of
the ghetto and the repression of the underground rising,
and of the sombre epilogue of annihilation wreaked on the
entire city. But he has seen the relics of these horrors. Much
nearer to him was Auschwitz, where the furnaces worked
incessantly to reduce a whole people to ashes. He has often
visited this scene of evil, after Calvary one of the most terrible spots on earth.

In those years Polish resilience, which is legendary, was
stretched to the limit. It still sufficed. Young people, university students like Karol Wojtyla, had to work and carry
an *arbeitskarte* if they were to escape the SS or Gestapo
net, and whatever fate a brutal commander would decree.

Wojtyla went to work in a stone quarry at Zakrzow outside Krakow. Hewing stones in conditions of such abject
misery as surrounded him would scarcely appear inspiring.
Yet in later years when the quarry labourer had turned to
different occupations it inspired his poetry. One of these

poems, "The Stone Quarry", starting from the physical, somewhat repellent details of the daily toil rises to visions of human power, interweaves ideals of human self-mastery with the hard task of conquering stone, speaks of love as a dynamic in life.

The workman rose a degree higher in the labour-force when he changed to the Solway chemical factory in Krakow. He told 2,500 workers gathered in Rome on 9 December 1978:

> For a short period of my life during the last world war I, too, had personal experience of factory work. I know what the task of daily labour means to those dependent on others. I know its dullness and monotony: I know the needs of the working class, their just demands and their lawful aspirations. And I know how necessary it is that work should never be a thing to alienate and frustrate, but should match the higher spiritual dignity of man.

Wojtyla seems to have been able to achieve some ascendancy over his work-mates without arousing jealousy of his better education. He used what advantage he had over them to help them, organising a recreation and cultural centre inside the factory. Soon he had made a decision which stirred genuine sympathy on their part: he decided to become a priest. Their sympathy was practical: they took on part of his factory work so that he should be free to study.

But he had not easily abandoned the hope of a future in the theatre. He was, during the German occupation, a member of the Rhapsodic Theatre (Teatr Rapsodyczny) as was his friend Kotlarczyk. The motivation was patriotic and artistic. Meetings for verse readings and performance of verse dramas were perforce clandestine. Themes chosen were nationalistic and favourite authors were Polish, like Wyspianski, whose play "The Wedding" was very popular.

A Polish prelate has stated that young Karol Wojtyla did some work for the resistance movement. Joseph Lichten, representative in Rome of the American Jewish Association, B'nai B'rith, issued a statement soon after the papal election on what Wojtyla did during the Jewish massacre. As an active participant in a clandestine relief organisation, Unia, he had given assistance to Jews in the Krakow area. He helped them to find hiding-places, saving them from deportation and death. When, after the war, he himself could come out of hiding, he identified with the remnant of the Wadowice Jewish community, reduced to just 500 persons and was active in restoring their cemetery in the town. He has been a lifelong friend of one member of the Wadowice community, Jerzy Kluger, whose father was president of this decimated ethnic group. Kluger has gone to the Vatican and been cordially received by the Pope. Another boyhood friend of the Pope's, Jezy Zubrzycki, a university professor in Australia, has a similar memory of Wojtyla's compassion and help for the stricken Jews. On 12 March, 1979, Pope John Paul II received a Jewish delegation and addressed them at length on the task of joint understanding called for between the two religions; he stressed the immense debt of Christianity to Old Testament Judaism.

To the Pope himself is attributed the story of his decision to become a priest. Once, when visiting a very poor family in the parish of St Florian's, where for a while he served as parish priest, he was so touched by their misery — an invalid father, a mother trying to provide for four children — that he shared with them the only possession he had at the time, the memory of a great grace from almighty God. He had been in two accidents, once when he was knocked down by a tram and badly concussed — when, allegedly, he was given a better memory — the second time when hit by a truck. In the mental disturbance following the first accident he saw one thing clearly: he was called to the priesthood. He resisted through his love for the theatre. Again, after his second mishap, the call came to him. This time he answered it.

Behind this painful experience and its happy outcome there is another factor, the influence of a saintly friend. In his early twenties, Wojtyla met a saintly layman, Jan Tyranowski, a tailor, a man who liked to read St John of

the Cross, the Spanish doctor of mystical theology, whom he
recommended to Wojtyla and the few others who had
gathered around him. That Wojtyla found the Spanish
mystic not only readable, but congenial, itself tells us
something of his spiritual development. There was one
affinity between the future Pope and the Spanish theologian: John of the Cross is a poet's poet and Karol was sensitive to poetry.

A survivor of the Rhapsodic Theatre, Sofia Kotlarczyk,
has told of the surprise they got when Wojtyla, cast in an
important role in a forthcoming production, informed them
that he could not play it as he had decided to enter the
seminary. He had discussed the question with the Archbishop of Krakow, Adam Sapieha, who had advised him to
begin seminary studies while continuing to work in the
Solway factory. The young man was very much on his
own, as his father had died in 1941. It is believed that he
really wished to enter the religious order of St John of the
Cross, the Carmelites. The archbishop advised him to post-
pone that decision and accept the only seminary training
then available in Krakow.

Adam Sapieha had then, and until his death, a strong influence in the life of the future John Paul II. The archbishop
has a notable place in the history of the Church in Poland
in the time of its most testing ordeal. Seventy-fifth occupant
of the See of Krakow he was, like his predecessors, an aris-
tocrat, a prince, a man of broad culture, discerning in
spiritual matters, a man with strong nerves. He needed them.
He had worked for ten years in the Roman Curia under St
Pius X who appointed him bishop and remained his hero.
He then came to know Mgr Eugenio Pacelli, the future Pius
XII. Sapieha's letters to Pius are among the most illumina-
ting in the large two-volume collection of Vatican war
documents dealing with Poland. They express profound
admiration and compassion for the man from whom others
easily asked the impossible.

Sapieha was seventy-two when the war broke out. In
February of that year he had asked to be relieved of his

office, on grounds of ill-health. He was persuaded to remain on by Pius XII who became Pope on 2 March. Cardinal Hlond, Primate of Poland, was in exile during the war so the Archbishop of Krakow was the acknowledged church leader. He was at the centre of the storm that beat incessantly on his country and its religion. He never flinched. To have lived under such a mighty leader was in itself a priceless education. To educate is to inspire or it is little. Sapieha was a man to inspire.

The archbishop's seminary, like all others, was closed. He improvised courses discreetly, accommodating teachers and students in rooms at the rear of the episcopal residence. The offices of the well-known Catholic publications *Tygodnik Powszechny* and *Znak* are situated there today. There the students came in the evening to study theology. For Karol it was one kind of clandestine exercise in place of another. This was his preparation for the priesthood, from 1942 until the Red Army entered Krakow in 1945. When the University reopened, he followed the course in the theology faculty there as a diocesan seminarist. He was lucky to have survived the Nazi terror. He had been on a wanted list and the Archbishop had kept him in close hiding for five months.

Sapieha was named Cardinal by Pius XII in the large postwar promotion to the Sacred College. While in Rome in 1946 for the ceremonies, he inquired about accommodation for two seminarists whom he had chosen for advanced studies. The Polish College in Rome was still closed. Two places were available in the Belgian seminary. The Cardinal ordained Karol Wojtyla priest on 1 November that year in the Wawel Cathedral and sent him with a fellow priest to the Belgian seminary in Rome.

Before dealing with young Fr Wojtyla's student days in Rome, we must consider particularly painful questions in recent Polish Catholicism because the personalities involved were close to him. One was the Cardinal who had guided his steps to the priesthood and would give him every opportunity to develop his many talents. The other was Pope Pius

XII. He named Wojtyla bishop and, in the whirligig of time, it is Wojtyla, now Pope John Paul II, who will be the highest judge in the cause of Pius XII's beatification, which has already been introduced.

Did Pius XII do all that he could for the Polish Catholics who were victims of the Nazi fury? As a young man John Paul II lived through the fury. The evil from which he and his fellow Catholics in Poland suffered was more than that. There was an elaborate plan for the systematic elimination of the Catholic Church. The programme was quickly drawn up after the successful German invasion. All the Polish provinces bordering on Germany were declared annexed to the Reich. One part, the largest, which included a number of important dioceses, was set up as a separate administrative province, the Reichsgau Wartheland or Warthegau, named from the river Wartha which flows through the region. This arbitrarily created province contained 4,600,000 inhabitants. It was chosen for the pilot scheme which would be applied in all German-controlled lands, eventually in the Reich itself. The plan included thorough Germanisation with a national church independent of Rome. Arthur Greiser, former president of Gdansk Senate, was put in charge of the Warthegau, with direct access to Hitler over the Berlin ministries. Reports of cruel persecution would reach the Vatican from this area in particular for Greiser carried out his orders with inhuman efficiency. But from everywhere in Poland the news was painful, distressing, increasingly bitter.

What was the Pope to do and say? He could do very little for the Poles inside the country because his relief schemes were blocked. The Pontifical Aid Commission, which covered a vast area and channeled immense financial and material help, was not allowed to enter German-occupied territory. The Pontifical Information Service set up to trace prisoners lost to their families had, likewise, very little success within the Nazi orbit.

The Poles at home and abroad still looked for papal support of a different kind. In the first months of the war they had been happy with the Pope's response. He had spoken words of comfort and encouragement to the Polish colony in Rome and, at the request of Hlond, had written words of sympathy in his first Encyclical: "But already death, devastation, mourning, calamity have overtaken countless families. The blood of so many cruelly slaughtered, though they bore no military rank, cries to heaven especially from the well-loved land of Poland." Pius went on to praise Poland's past glories and her trust in Our Lady as "she waits for the day when peace and justice will be restored, the day when she will be allowed at last to emerge unharmed from the waves that have engulfed her". Talks from Vatican Radio were in a similar vein.

But as the war continued the Pope seemed to go silent. Many messages reached him asking for an outright condemnation of the Nazi persecution. Among those urging such a pronouncement were the exiled Polish president, Raczkiewicz, the country's ambassador to the Holy See, Casimir Papee, a bishop who could not return to his diocese and was resident in England, Radonski of Wloclawek, not to mention diplomats in Rome who wanted the Pope as a piece of propaganda.

From Poland itself voices spoke differently. A German bishop in Poznan, appointed provisionally and, in the chaotic conditions of the time, accepted by the Polish bishops, Hilary Breitinger, O.F.M., told Pius that protests against his silence were coming from the faithful. Sapieha, whose two secretaries were taken off to concentration camps and whose correspondence was intercepted by the Gestapo, as late as 1942 wrote thus to the Pope: "We much deplore that we cannot communicate Your Holiness's letters to the faithful but that would provide a pretext for fresh persecution and we already have those who have been victimised because they were suspected of being in secret communication with the Apostolic See."

The Germans, as Breitinger to his honour pointed out, were taunting and tormenting the Poles with the idea that the Pope knew what was being done and by his silence approved. This was an intolerable burden of sorrow. It was brought into the Pope's own bureau by a Polish nun, Mother Laureta Lubowidzka, Superior General of the Sisters of Nazareth. Pius told her of his love for her country and asked her did the Poles believe enemy propaganda to the contrary. She said that some did. "Write to them and tell them not to believe it, because the Pope has much love for Poland. This is the truth, it is the truth, it is the truth." The nun immediately went on Vatican Radio and broadcast what the Pope had told her.

The official papers now released in Germany and Rome show an interminable string of protests from the Vatican to the Nazi government. They culminated in the 5,000 word denunciation of the horrors committed in the Warthegau, which was delivered at the Foreign Ministry in Berlin in March 1943. The Poles knew nothing of all this. At the Nuremberg trials, Ribbentrop spoke of it as a "deskful of protests" received from Rome. The Poles did not know that these Vatican memoranda would be used in evidence against the Germans at Nuremberg. Above all they did not know that one reason why Hitler persistently refused to heed any criticism, request or condemnation of his policy in their country made by Pius XII was that the Pope refused absolutely to recognise the German annexation of Polish territory.

Pius relied on Sapieha's judgement. When, in 1943, the archbishop asked him to speak out in public, but in such a way that persons in Poland would not be involved as recipients of a papal message, he decided to broadcast in June of that year words of support for the nation, of praise for the merits of "its saints and heroes, its scholars and thinkers", of condemnation of all evil acts committed on Polish soil, of prayer "for a future in harmony with the rightness of Polish aspirations and the greatness of Polish sacrifices."

Thereafter the bonds between the Poles and Pius XII became once again close and strong. He gave a special blessing to the armed forces at the request of their chaplain general, Bishop Joseph Gawlina; twice he received large contingents of soldiers with their officers in the Vatican. His letter of thanks to General Anders for a beautiful presentation made to him by the military delegation is the only letter from a Pope to a commander in the field in modern times — it appeared in the *Acta Apostolicae Sedis*. Pius transmitted at once to the British Minister to the Vatican the most poignant document of the second world war, the telegram sent to him by the women of Warsaw *in extremis*, which ended with the words:

> Holy Father no one is helping us. The Russian armies which have been for three weeks at the gates of Warsaw have not advanced a step. The aid coming to us from Great Britain is insufficient. The world is ignorant of our fight. God alone is with us. Holy Father, Vicar of Christ, if you can hear us bless us Polish women who are fighting for the Church and for freedom.

The war over, Archbishop Sapieha, now in his seventy-ninth year, enjoyed the prestige of a national hero; gone were the days when he would pointedly offer the German governor who called on him, Hans Frank, the meagre ersatz coffee, beetroot jam and black bread on which he and his fellow Poles had to survive. Sir Francis d'Arcy Osborne, British Minister to the Vatican, relayed to the Holy See, after the conclusion of hostilities, a message received from the British embassy in Moscow, at the time the nearest listening-post to Poland:

> The provisional authorities have also been at great pains to conciliate the Catholic Hierarchy. For example at a recent meeting in Krakow in honour of General Zymierski, Archbishop Sapieha was treated with great honour and held up as a model Pole who had shown outstanding qualities in resisting the German invaders.

Sapieha had fully understood Pius XII's agonizing problem. Pius feared immediate, terrible reprisals on innocent victims if he did what many wished him to do, publish a denunciation of Nazi crimes. In the detached atmosphere of the Nuremberg courtroom one witness after another gave evidence of this aspect of Hitler's character. He reacted violently when contradicted or opposed. The victims of the concentration camps knew it by experience. They suffered when Church authorities denounced the iniquities of the regime. Dutch Catholic Jews, among them Edith Stein, paid with their lives for the outspoken words of the hierarchy — in Holland there was the highest proportion of Jewish deaths in any Nazi dependency.

We are not putting ideas into Pius XII's head in expressing this judgement. He himself explained his dilemma to the College of Cardinals:

> Every word on our part, addressed on this subject to the competent authorities, every public allusion had to be seriously weighed and measured by us, in the interests of the suffering themselves, so as not to render their lot, in spite of our wish, still more serious and unbearable. Alas, the improvements apparently obtained are in scale far from the maternal solicitude of the Church, on behalf of the particular groups that are subject to the most cruel fate; and as Jesus before his own city as to cry out in sorrow, *Quoties volui . . . et noluisti* (Lk 13:34), so his Vicar, though he asked only for pity and sincere return to the elementary laws of justice and humanity, has often found himself before doors which no key could open.

The Pope expressed the same sentiment and conviction in the Encyclical to the Russians in 1952 — there are also utterly reliable testimonies in relation to his private conversations during the war in which he spoke similarly.

In the other parallel tragedy of the time, the Jewish massacre, Pius XII's conduct was determined by the same over-riding consideration. He had read *Mein Kampf.* He knew why Hitler wished to destroy the Jewish race. He knew how hopeless were appeals to the Fuhrer, for when his nuncio went to Berchtesgaden to plead for the Jews, Hitler took up a wine glass and smashed it on the floor; he never uttered a word.

The Vicar of Christ went as far as he possibly could in public utterance, for he must make his moral position clear. At Christmas, 1942, he spoke these words which have escaped a number of his critics:

> Humanity owes this vow [to bring back society to divine law . . . with a view to the service of the human person

and of a divinely ennobled human order] to those hundreds of thousands who, without any fault of their own, sometimes only by reason of their nationality or race, are marked down for death or progressive extinction.

In the following June, on the day he spoke of the Poles, Pius referred again to his concern for those

who turn to us the gaze of anxious entreaty tormented as they are, because of their nationality or their race, by greater evils, by sorrows more acute and heavier, delivered, without any fault on their part, to measures of extermination.

Poland before the war had over 3,000,000 Jews; after the war there were about 40,000. Most of these dead had perished in the death camps of Auschwitz, Majdanek and Treblinka. Pius XII could do nothing for them. The allied powers could have rescued many, but took no measures at all except to make threatening pronouncements on what would happen to the criminals *after* the war; they did not even reply to the simple request to bomb the railway line to Auschwitz, a measure which could have saved many lives.

What Pius XII did in areas where he had some freedom to help the Jews has now been fully documented by Jewish writers like Jeno Levai, Pinhas Lapide and David Hirsteg. Through his nuncios, long before the massacre started, in one country after another, he protested against anti-Jewish legislation. When he could gain a hearing, as with Admiral Horthy of Hungary, he pleaded for cessation of the killings or the deportations which led to these: he sent Horthy an open telegram and Horthy answered favourably.

A vast rescue operation all over Europe got under way and everyone knew that this was the Pope's most ardent wish. Lapide sums up the result as 860,000 lives saved, more than by any other agency, institution or government, more than by all others together. Those who say that Pius XII said nothing in this appalling matter err; those who say he did nothing err on a gigantic scale.

How much all that touched the young Karol Wojtyla at the time we do not know. It was in the midst of such utterly unprecedented happenings that he reached the years of early manhood. The local effects of the policy of frightfulness that he witnessed make up his memory of that terrible time. This memory he took to Rome, the Rome of Pius XII. Life in that city, to which he would return very frequently in the years ahead, gave him an opportunity to learn Italian. It enriched him culturally as it does anyone sensitive to a unique legacy of the spirit. In the Belgian College he came in contact with another tradition and learned another language. The future Pope during those years met for the first time the Polish diaspora. He met expatriate Poles like Archbishop Gawlina, who, freed from his military duties, was named Ordinary, that is bishop in charge, of all Polish exiles.

Those who visited Rome during the years 1946 and 1947, as did the present writer, will have a memory of lassitude, confusion and widespread anxiety. If the young Karol Wojtyla saw in the military cemeteries of Monte Cassino, Loreto and Bologna evidence of his fellow-countrymen's valour in death, he could be forgiven for asking himself had they died in vain. In Italy the political atmosphere was full of menace. The communists did not have an over-all majority in parliament, but they were the largest single party and in Togliatti they had a leader with remarkable ability and drive. The Pope's own village, Castlegandolfo, elected a communist municipal council; party slogans could be seen on the walls of the Vatican. Italian communists, moreover, were tied to the ruling clique in Moscow and accepted Stalin's dictate.

The Russian dictator saw his opportunity in Europe wither during the ominous year 1947. In April 1948, Italy refused an electoral mandate to the communist party. A halting hesitant recovery was under way. In the moment of crisis the personality of Pius XII had been the decisive factor. He went on thereafter to a new shining phase in his career, the huge assemblies, the specially convened international groups of the 1950s, the erudite, eloquent texts and discourses in half-a-dozen languages on an encyclopedic range of subjects. We have not yet heard any word about

him from John Paul II but after the consecration of Archbishop of Maharski, his successor in the See of Krakow, he
sent as a special gift to the Cathedral Chapter of the city
the picture of Our Lady of Czestochowa which had been
presented to Pius XII on 3 May 1943 by General Sikorski,
then the exiled president of Poland.

Karol Wojtyla's memory of catastrophe in his homeland
or awareness of disturbing signs of the times in Italy did not
deflect him from his work. On 27 November 1946, he was
enrolled in the Faculty of Theology of the Angelico, at that
time a Pontificium Athenaeum, now a university, directed
and staffed by the Dominicans. On 2 July 1947, he obtained
the Licentiate in Theology *summa cum laude,* that is with
the highest possible distinction. In the following year,
1947-1948, he followed the doctorate course. He studied
under Fr Reginald Garrigou-Lagrange, a prestigious name in
pre-conciliar Catholic theology. "Garrigou" as he was so
often called, a close friend of Jacques Maritain, industrious,
prolific, widely translated, taught dogmatic theology and
held a chair, which he had founded, in ascetical and mystical
theology. He was a leading spirit in *La Vie Spirituelle* and
La Vie Intellectuelle, reviews which to those of an older
generation represent a whole world of Catholicism emerging
to fill a vital role in the modern age.

Sympathy between French and Poles is innate on each
side. The subject of Wojtyla's doctoral dissertation "Faith
in the teaching of St John of the Cross", deepened the
sympathy between him and his gifted teacher. On 19 June
1948, he defended his thesis successfully. The other
assessor who acted with his professor was Fr. Philippe.

During the summer holidays from academic work, Fr
Wojtyla was directed, doubtless by Archbishop Gawlina, to
minister among the expatriate Polish communities in Europe,
some particularly isolated and suffering, as in the aftermath
of the war they could not return to their own country. The
young priest took advantage of his stay in France and Belgium to study the J.O.C. (Young Christian Workers) and its
various offshoots, J.A.C., J.E.C.. When he was in Paris he

stayed in the Polish Seminary, in the Rue des Irlandais, the Irish College in Paris, founded four hundred years ago and placed at the disposal of the Poles by the Irish bishops after the war. In his subsequent visits to the French capital up to the time of his election as Pope he generally stayed in the Irish College.

Equipped thus with learning and experience, Fr Wojtyla was ready to return to Krakow. Some of his teachers and directors he would meet again, in circumstances none could foresee. The rector of the Belgian Seminary, Mgr Fürstenberg, became a Cardinal, as did the assessor of his doctorate thesis, Fr Philippe. His professors at the Angelico had been Frs Deandrea, Duncker, Gillon, Luigi Ciappi and Michael Browne. Of these the last two also became Cardinals. Fr Browne was first to hold the offices of Master of the Sacred Palace, that is official theologian to the Pope, and Master General of the Dominican Order. Few future Popes have had a cluster of future cardinals so close about them.

3   The Stalinists

If Stalin had missed his coup in western Europe, he twisted
the screw all the more tightly on his empire in the east.
Some years had been needed in Russia and the satellite
countries for rebuilding and restoration of indispensable
services such as transport. The tyrant then felt that the
plan of subjugation could be drawn up and put into effect.
His servants in the different countries were at the height of
their power and ruthlessness between 1951 and 1956, for
though the master died in 1953 he was not publicly dis-
owned until three years later. Why after a war declared to
liberate the Poles they should be handed over to Stalin is
for historians of Yalta and Potsdam to explain. Supported
by these treaties the Russian ruler had no difficulty in im-
posing his men on the country. They set up a regime which
accepted strong political, economic and military links with
Moscow and controlled everything with the apparatus of a
police state. Not a police state of the worst kind, however.
There has never been anything in Poland like the AVH
Hungarian police whose infamy in Andrassy Street, Buda-
pest, was revealed to the world in 1956.

The Polish Stalinists worked against the Church to a pat-
tern which was, in its essentials, uniform all over eastern
Europe. The programme was carried out in phases. First,
outside ecclesiastical help — given by Apostolic Nuncios for
example — was blocked. Then, all institutions affecting public opinion were removed from the Church's control, as were
all its assets, charitable or cultural. Show trials or summary
detention were used to separate bishops from people and to
demoralise the clergy. Finally, associations of "progressive

Catholics" were fostered to detach leading Catholics from the hierarchy and tie them to the regime. These people were favoured in many ways, by liberal supplies of paper for example for their publications — paper, as all other important commodities, is under government control.

These measures, pressures, techniques were painstakingly used against Polish Catholicism. Why did they not succeed? Why was the Church in this country to come forth after three decades not only as the strongest in eastern Europe, but one of the strongest in the world? Why does one see such crowds in the churches? How does one explain the figures for priestly ordinations in recent years, 1974, 638; 1975, 606; 1976, 477; 1977, 438; 1978, 595? Why does Poland have 5,000 seminarists whereas France with one and a half times the population has but 1,000? The different seminaries in the city of Krakow, those of the diocese and of two other dioceses, Katowice and Czestochowa, and ten directed by religious orders and congregations, have altogether 1,000 seminarists.

Recent surveys show that the picture is not uniformly bright, that church attendance and attitudes to ecclesiastical authority even on matters like abortion, on which the bishops have taken an exemplary stand, vary through different social and intellectual levels. Yet the survival of the Catholic body as an entity, public, dominant in the country, is a complete reversal of the ordinary laws of history. This is a theme for a great Church historian.

He will note that population movements favoured Catholics. Losses in the east and west raised the proportion of Catholics from 75 per cent to over 90 per cent of the whole population — one must allow for the loss of over three million Jews in the gas chambers.

Another decisive factor was the close cohesion of the hierarchy. Every effort to split them failed miserably. This was tried as late as 1967 when the Archbishop of Krakow was named Cardinal. He was to be the favourite of the regime in contrast to the hard, unbending Wyszynski. In his speech of acceptance in Rome and in another on his return to Poland he scotched any such hope.

As the Pope said in his letter to the Polish people after his election he would not be where he is today without Wyszynski. For in post-war Poland this one man embodied the whole people through every religious crisis.

Inside the whole communist world, from east Berlin to the China Sea, from Siberia to the Dalmatian coast, there is no figure quite comparable to Stefan Wyszynski, in the sixty-one years since the Russian Revolution. It was Karol Wojtyla's good fortune to share his ideals, to live under his protecting shadow, to be his collaborator as a bishop, his partner as a Cardinal. The Primate has not the sparkling talents of the younger man, nor his flair for human contacts, nor his out-door interests — one cannot imagine him skiing in the Tatra mountains or canoeing. He has not left Poland as often as Wojtyla who travelled, through the generosity of the Polish diaspora, twice to North America, in 1969 and in 1976, to Australia in 1973, to Latin America, to the Philippines and New Guinea, to very many European countries, to East and West Germany, to France several times, and to Italy so often in recent years that there was a joke current in Krakow that he had a monthly ticket to Rome.

When Wyszynski was leaving Rome after his first visit as a Cardinal in 1957 he spoke a memorable word: "Pray for us, we are holding the rampart." That has been his destiny. For that he needed three things: faith, strength, power with God. His faith is manifest in every word he speaks. It is faith properly instructed, versed in the conditions of the time. After studies at Lublin University he was sent to Rome, France, Germany, Belgium and Holland for further courses. He edited a priests' paper for a while, taught in a seminary and was at the same time involved with Trade Unions. He founded a Workers' University. That was all immediately be-fore the war. During the war, in Lublin and Warsaw, he con-ducted clandestine lectures, was ready to take over the direction of Wlockawek Seminary when hostilities ceased and was named soon afterwards Bishop of Lublin. That was in 1946, the year of Wojtyla's ordination. Two years later Wyszynski was Primate.

His power before men has been shown in the word. He is a mighty orator clear, cogent, simple in style, ranging over many subjects especially on the human tragedies which have occurred in his country. He has spoken many times to gatherings of priests, ex-prisoners of Dachau. His publications altogether, mostly oratorical, make a bibliography of over 500 items.

The driving power has been an intrepid spirit. "We encourage you", wrote Paul VI to the Primate in 1974 for the fiftieth anniversary of his priestly ordination, "who are hardened in courage and confident in the might of the holy name of Jesus and the victorious Cross, to continue working for the Church." The Pope drew attention in the same letter to something which is so well known about Wyszynski as to be an assumption by those who know him, his singular devotion to the Blessed Virgin Mary.

He succeeded Hlond as Primate in 1949 and could expect the same rough treatment that was meted out to others inside the communist orbit who held similar office: in eastern Europe Stepinac, Beran, Mindszenty. He was to survive to lead the College of Cardinals to the feet of a Polish Pope, an outcome that was not foreseen in the plans of the communists. Even his survival to his present age, seventy-eight, would have been thought utterly impossible on the day of his ordination, so sickly did he then appear. Someone said he looked a better candidate for a cemetery than for Holy Orders.

From the beginning of the battle between Church and State for the soul of the nation, the bishops led by Wyszynski did not opt out or choose an aloof stance. Even in the darkening days of 1950 they reached a formal agreement with the government, which in 1946 had repudiated the Concordat of 1925. The 1946 agreement was in seventeen articles with a supplementary protocol in four articles. It was signed by W. Wolski, Minister for Education, by General Edward Ochab, Vice-Minister for Defence and on the Church's side by Bishop Choromanski, secretary to the episcopate, and two other bishops. The bishops promised that the clergy "within the limits of its pastoral office would teach the faithful respect for the laws and for the State authorities" and, in a concession which at the time was thought excessive, they accepted this proposition: "The principle that the Pope is the supreme and decisive authority in the Church relates to questions of faith and morals and also to matters of ecclesiastical jurisdiction. In all other affairs the hierarchy will act in conformity with the political interests of the State." The bishops would support the government's claim to the western territories.

In exchange the Church received a great deal related to its mission: guarantees in regard to religious education and Catholic schools, freedom for Catholic associations, for works of charity and for the Catholic press and Catholic publications. Public manifestations of piety would not be hindered; pastoral ministry to the army, in prisons and in hospitals would be allowed; religious orders and congregations would "within the limits imposed by their vocation and by laws at present in force" enjoy complete freedom of action.

It was all on paper and the paper was soon torn up. Ochab, a month after the agreement was signed, declared publicly: "Half measures and evasive insinuations will be useless and injurious . . . because we Marxists will continue to intensify our watchfulness in accordance with the realism propounded by Marx, Engels, Lenin and Stalin."

Night came down again on the homeland of Wyszynski and Wojtyla. Once again the Poles were alone. Bishops were imprisoned, as was the Cardinal. He was not, however, tortured as was Mindszenty. Hundreds of priests were detained or deported. Catholic publications were practically wiped out. Religion was banished from the schools. The giant Catholic organisation, Caritas, which dispensed assistance and relief through hundreds of institutions, was taken over by the State. In every office of government service, unrelenting discrimination was practised against committed

Catholics. The country was saturated with militant Marxist propaganda.

To launch and maintain a movement of "progressive" Catholics the government found a willing ally in one of the enigmatic and baneful figures of post-war Poland, a pre-war fascist turned Marxist, a man of tireless energy with consummate skill in diplomatic manoeuvre, Boleslaw Piasecki. He founded the "Pax" movement, which over the years caused pain to Catholics at home and confusion abroad and sought, unsuccessfully despite enormous financial subsidy, to split the Catholic body, in particular to alienate the laity from the bishops.

Piasecki's life was marked by tragedy. His first wife was killed in the Warsaw Rising. His eldest son was found stabbed to death through the heart, macabre symbolism that has been differently interpreted. He was himself captured by the Russians and condemned to death. Inexplicably, the sentence was quashed and within a short time the " eastern pretender" was confirmed in a position of unique power. A Stalinist in the government sponsored the deal by which the Pax leader held a monopoly of Catholic publishing and Catholic art sales. Pax ran the only Catholic daily, *Slowo Powszechne* and for a while was given control also of the well-known Catholic weekly, *Tygodnik Powszechny*. Piasecki was a capitalist operating freely within the communist system: favours and privileges were heaped upon him; his daily was sometimes allowed paper for 200,000 copies; he had ten other publications. Intelligent, well-informed, Catholic Poles confess that the man was an enigma. In the Stalinist days he followed the government line. Using such titles as "Committee of Catholic Intellectuals" or "movement of progressive Catholics" he worked with the State Security Office, U.B.. Pax was, at the time, a front for the police state. When the Cardinal and bishops were interned, Piasecki published a book which attempted to plan the Church's role in the new order, *Essential Problems*: bishops and the Cardinal must understand the changing socio-political situation!

Piasecki had another side, which was more manifest after the fall of the Stalinists, when he had lost an empire and was looking for a role. He submitted to the decree of the Holy Office which had put his book on the Index. When his weekly, *Dzis i Jutro* ("Today and Tomorrow"), was condemned by Rome he dropped publication of it and issued *Kierunki* in its place. In 1956 two of his delegates in Rome could announce that Pax had published altogether three million copies of Catholic works. This momentum was continued; the titles often included important foreign works by Catholic authors.

The eastern pretender turned increasingly to Catholic practice in his last years and months. He never recaptured the position he had held before the 1956 thaw, but his emissaries abroad, especially in France, caused great confusion about the Church in Poland. As late as 1963 the Vatican Secretary of State, Cardinal Villot, had to communicate to the Paris Nuncio a memorandum by Cardinal Wyszynski on the real nature of Pax. It was for distribution among French bishops, some of whom had been perplexed by the plausible propaganda of Polish fellow-travellers. At the time, the editor in chief of *Slowo Powszechne,* Dankowski, had been eloquent on the contrast between the diehard Polish bishops and the liberal John XXIII.

Inside Poland, however, Wyszynski had the situation well in hand. Clerical participation in Pax had fallen to nothing — when a commemoration ceremony was organised shortly before Piasecki's death in January 1979 no priest could be found to attend, let alone speak, and a Hungarian priest was brought on. Priest membership of Pax in Poland was never on the scale of that in the other eastern European countries. In the first years amid spreading confusion and the general disarray of Catholic forces produced by the imprisonment policy, meetings of the "Patriot Priests" and "Peace Priests" were attended by upwards of 1,000 priests and laity. Deceit and intimidation were used and, in known cases, priests were dragooned to such assemblies. Less than three weeks after the Cardinal's arrest a national congress of patriot priests took place in Warsaw. It was decided to set up a "Central Committee of the National Front of Progressive Priests and Laymen". This was a body of sixty-five members, clerical and lay, formed to "cement and strengthen the unity of the nation".

Priests collaborating in these manoeuvres were favourites of the regime, assured preferential treatment where political influence was possible. Some of them were forced on bishops as Vicars General. Some seminarists, too, were suborned to report on proceedings within the seminaries. It is difficult to ascertain exact numbers of the clergy fully involved in the scheme: possibly thirty of forty in 1950, rising to 100 in 1953 and declining rapidly after that.

Piasecki died on 4 January 1979. Wyszynski, magnanimous as ever, sent a special message of sympathy to his relatives and had his Vicar General celebrate Mass in public for the deceased publicist. He promised to say Mass privately for the man who had caused him very much trouble and embarrassment. A concelebrant of the public Mass was the poet priest, Twardowski, who had bestowed spiritual comfort on the dying man.

Faced with Stalinist oppression and repression, the Polish laity had early discovered a simple law which worked infallibly: you cannot put the whole town in jail. If they all went to church there was nothing the secret police could do save attend and report on what the priest had said. The collective witness was given epoch-making expression on 26 August 1956. On that day more than a million people, despite widespread economic misery and restrictions of every kind, with only makeshift transport, many having walked for days, converged like a mighty sea at the hearthstone of Polish Catholicism, Czestochowa. A whole people had thrown down the gauntlet to the enemies of their faith. Someone then said: "If there is a God in heaven this nation must have a glorious future."

That was a year of tumult inside eastern Europe. Tito had already shown that the Stalinist monolith could be cracked. The idol was next dethroned in his own country.

Khruschev had, at the twentieth party congress in March, utterly demolished the Stalin myth. Poland was seething with rage and discontent which no longer could be contained. An incompetent government, economically subservient to Moscow, had reduced the population to penury, in places to near starvation, and in June the workers had rioted in Poznan during the industrial fair: a protest hitherto unheard of inside the communist world.

Two things were urgent in this state of universal tension. The ruling clique must be ejected and the enthusiasts must be restrained. Poland could not afford a blood-bath like that which the Hungarians went through. Someone thought of Gomulka, a dissident, a man once in deep trouble with the hard-liners. He had been imprisoned by Beirut and on release had slept with a revolver under his pillow. He was now set up as Party Secretary and, with his chosen lieutenants, supervised the thaw of the cold war. On 28 October, it was announced that the Cardinal had been set free. A week later five interned bishops were released. Catholic intellectuals who had been victimised established a club for mutual support. The Catholic press was allowed some measure of independent existence. The Pax monopoly was broken.

In 1948 Fr Karol Wojtyla returned to work in Poland. The regime would see to it that he had little scope for social work of the kind that he had studied in the French and Belgian Young Christian Worker movement. Cardinal Sapieha at first seemed to provide little scope for his intellectual progress, although he seemed destined for the academic world, his scholarly attainments being of the highest. His first appointment was to a country curacy in the village of Niegowice, near Wieliczka.

Living conditions in the immediate aftermath of the war were meagre. The young curate who arrived one day at Niegowice was fully adapted to this state of affiars. He came with a small suitcase and with a big heart as the peasants in the adjoining countryside soon discovered to their joy. He was available to all, especially to those in difficulty or with problems. Rough transport on wooden carts was quite acceptable, when he did not make his pastoral visitations on foot. And immediately his oratorical gift, the fine voice which had made him so popular as an actor, bound people to him.

Later, to the great sorrow of the villagers, he was changed to a city parish in Krakow, St Florian's. Again some of the faithful were disconcerted when their reception committee nearly missed him because he made the journey from Niegowice on a wooden cart with very light luggage. His cassock looked shabby and got worse as time passed. But the parishioners soon realised that, after God, he was entirely dedicated to them. His habits of prayer, his hours in the chapel before the Blessed Sacrament, his whole bearing as a priest and his fidelity to duty were, for people in need of spiritual support, the things that really counted.

He is remembered for his interest in people, his easy manner, his readiness when visiting his parishioners around Christmas time to join in carol singing. He is remembered, above all as a captivating preacher of the word of God. People flocked to hear him, university students among them.

While engaged in pastoral ministry in St Florian's, Fr Wojtyla returned to university studies at Krakow University. Under the direction of Fr Wladyslaw Wicher, he prepared for the doctorate in theology, specialising in moral theology. This was but a preliminary to his real ambition, which was to devote a dissertation to a problem which fascinated him: the possibility of reconciling modern philosophy with the Thomism he had studied in Rome. One is reminded of the pioneering work accomplished by Cardinal Mercier in Louvain University.

To qualify for the degree of Agrégé of Krakow University, Wojtyla prepared a dissertation on the possibility of founding a Christian ethic on the system of Max Scheler. The work was defended in 1953. It appeared in print from the Press of the University of Lublin in 1959.

As a result of these advanced studies, Fr Wojtyla was transferred from parochial to academic work. First he taught moral theology and social ethics in the senior seminary of the diocese. Like all other similar institutions, it was under severe pressure and restriction. These were the worst years of Stalinism. In 1956, the year of the "thaw", he was named assistant professor at the Catholic University of Lublin, while retaining his post in Krakow. A year later, his status was raised to Professor Agrégé.

Lublin University is the only strictly Catholic institution of its kind between Milan and Formosa. Founded in 1918, it had grown steadily up to the outbreak of World War II. It was closed by the Germans. It was the first Polish university to reopen after the war. But as the regime turned hard and sour, the Catholic higher institute, by its very existence, was an irritant to the Marxists. It was victimised. All the faculties which could influence the social and economic life of the nation were suppressed. This left only the faculties of Theology, Christian Philosophy and Canon Law so that, in the worst days, student numbers had fallen to about 1,000. No state funds have ever been made available — unlike the Catholic Academy of Warsaw which, curiously, is financed by the State.

Lublin University lived, still lives, on money raised by the Church and on gifts from Associates of the University, who number over 200,000 — student fees are a tiny part of the annual income. The Bishop of Lublin is Chancellor and the committee responsible for Church aid is always headed by the Primate. Since the initial gift of 40,000 books transferred from the Catholic Academy of St Petersburg in 1918, the library has grown to impressive proportions, and has a fine department of scholarly reviews.

Fr Wojtyla commuted between Krakow and Lublin to keep his lecture engagements in the latter city. He travelled by train at night and worked through the hours he had thus to himself. For years he had been accustomed to curtailing his sleep apparently without any harmful effects on his health. Former pupils speak with admiration of his learning and his attractive style as a lecturer. Part of his duty was to conduct student seminars on the content of his courses. This brought him into contact with the students

individually and opened a wide field for his priestly apostolate. In encounters, excursions, cycling trips, he could identify with young people without losing their respect.

The university lecturer was not satisfied to meet the
needs of his immediate student audience. He accepted his
full responsibility as a Catholic academic. He did the research, undertook the reflection necessary to flesh out
scores of articles for scholarly reviews. Thus, too, was laid
the foundation for a lifelong regular intellectual output.
The large number of these articles appearing in 1957 —
nineteen in all — is explained by the changed political
climate. The *University Review* which carried Professor
Wojtyla's articles was restored to life late in 1956 and
appeared normally from 1957.

4 Bishop

Karol Wojtyla was one of the last bishops appointed by Pius XII. On 4 July 1958, when he was little over thirty-eight years of age, he was named to the titular See of Ombi and became Auxiliary Bishop of Krakow. The following 28 September he was consecrated by Eugeniusz Baziak, to whom he acted as Auxiliary. Baziak had been driven out by the Russians in 1945. In 1950, he was appointed Co-adjutor to Cardinal Sapieha. But when the Cardinal died the next year, he was appointed administrator rather than archbishop.

For the last four years of Baziak's life, Bishop Wojtyla worked with him. Then, on 17 May 1962, he was elected Vicar Capitular or acting Archbishop of Krakow. Pope Paul VI named him Archbishop Metropolitan of the historic diocese on 30 December 1963.

It is said the choice was between him, Mgr (later Cardinal) Filipiak who was in Rome, and a well-known Polish priest who was head of a nationwide charitable work for the blind. It is also said that the Government supported the candidature of Wojtyla, thinking that he would be more flexible, perhaps they even thought more pliant, than the old lion in Warsaw. They were to be so keenly disappointed in this hope that before the papal election their one fear was that Wojtyla himself would eventually come to Warsaw as Primate. The enthronement as Archbishop of Krakow took place on 8 March 1964, in the cathedral of Wawel.

Krakow had at that time a Catholic population of about a million and a half, with over 1,500 priests, secular and religious, about the same number of religious brothers and as many nuns. Wojtyla's humble origins had been little noticed heretofore. It could not escape attention that he was, as the seventy-sixth Ordinary of the ancient royal capital of Poland, the first commoner in the long line. His friend, Bishop Hnilica, the exiled Czech bishop — former inmate of concentration camps — has spoken of a kind of pride with which John Paul II remembers "the excessive distrust which, at the time of his appointment, his proletarian background aroused in certain traditionalist circles within his diocese". He had no complex about it nor reluctance to admit it. He invited to his episcopal ordination the workers of the Solway company's factory who had been kind to him when he worked with them.

The faithful of Krakow would, in time, learn that humble origins are no bar to religious and cultural distinction. The whole Church would tell them this about Cardinal Wojtyla, as it has told any who had similar misgivings about Cardinal Sarto of Venice who became St Pius X and Cardinal Roncalli of Venice who became John XXIII. With time, too, there grew a relationship between bishop and people which is best described in his own words:

> I bear all this in my heart and in a certain way keep it with me; my whole beloved Church of Krakow, a special part of Christ's Church in Poland and a special part of the history of our native land. Old and new Krakow, the new districts, the new people, the new suburbs, Nowa Huta: concern for the urgency of new churches and new parishes; the new needs of evangelisation, cathechesis and the apostolate. All this accompanies me on St Peter's Chair. All this constitutes a layer of my soul which I cannot leave. The layer of my experience, of my faith, of my love which expands to embrace so many places dear to me, so many sanctuaries of Christ and his Mother, such as Mogila, Ludmierz, Myslenic Staniatki or Rychwald and particularly Kalvaria Zebrzydowka with its paths along which I walked with such pleasure. I keep in my eyes and in my heart the panorama of the land of Krakow, Zywiec, Slask Podhale, Beskidy and Tatra. I offer to the Lord this beloved land and the whole landscape of Poland, but especially its people.

Kalvaria Zebrzydowka is a reproduction over a whole stretch

of rolling countryside near Krakow of the Way of the Cross. The future Pope frequently went there to pray, to follow its paths, to linger at the chapels erected there and to recall events from the Passion narrative.

If we are to attempt a character sketch of the man, now that as a bishop he was beginning his public career, his fully pastoral service, we should have to insist on his fidelity to prayer. It is surprising how many people who knew him for years say of him simply, "he is a man of prayer". One of his most familiar prayer patterns is characteristically Polish, addressed to the Blessed Virgin Mary. Those who would hear him pronounce before the image of Our Lady of Guadalupe a long moving prayer replete with doctrine and deep feeling would know that this was not an artifice of the moment but the fruit of prolonged contemplation, of a kind of communion between the author and his heavenly Mother. His episcopal coat of arms bore the letter M and the motto *Totus tuus,* "wholly yours", to signify his personal dedication, in the De Montfort manner, to Our Lady. In passing, the Poles are the only people committed publicly by their bishops in this way to Our Lady. In his public announcement from St Peter's of his acceptance of the papal office John Paul II twice invoked the Blessed Virgin Mary. He frequently applies to her the title Mother of the Church — for a reason that will be made clear later.

He is faithful to traditional devotions. Across the street from the episcopal palace in Krakow, in the Franciscan church, there is a special chapel of the Passion, with a miraculous Christ crucified and Stations of the Cross. John Paul II told his audience at Assisi when he went there on pilgrimage that he often made the Stations of the Cross in this church, and he has said in public in Rome that the Rosary is his favourite devotion.

On Karol Wojtyla's intellectual ability the judgement can be left to readers of his books and articles. When his work entitled *Love and Responsibility* appeared in French translation, the preface was written in flattering terms by Henri de Lubac, S.J., one of the giants of contemporary theology

— that was in 1965. Some admirers thought that the philosopher in him would produce ponderous, abstruse utterances once he became Pope. The voluminous pronouncements and writings which have already come from him allay any such fear.

One reason for this may have been the spirit of camaraderie which young and old, members of every profession, trade and party, so readily associate with the former Archbishop of Krakow. Generous, willing, even after his appointment as Archbishop, to remain as long as possible, until compelled to change, in a modest apartment where he was sought out by those in need, students very often, he had a distinctive kind of hospitality. Especially charged as he would be with the Lay Apostolate and living in a country where Catholic associations are banned, he improvised meetings. He would invite different groups to spend an evening with him, share an oplatek wafer, take a little wine and then engage in the earnest lively conversation that the Poles love: the subject, whatever happened to engage their lifework or interests directly. Such encounters had many effects, one being to give the churchman awareness of the need to communicate with people in their idiom, as simply as possible.

He was a very good listener. An Irish priest, Fr John Moriarty, who has had much to do with him in regard to the Legion of Mary, which he got to know in Paris through being invited by Cardinal Suenens to a Legion assembly, recalls especially the stillness that enveloped his person as he heard others speak. Jerzy Turowicz, editor of *Tygodnik Powszechny,* one of the most respected Catholic journalists in eastern Europe, a friend, almost a journalistic colleague of the future Pope, who often visited the editorial office and was a frequent contributor to the paper, gives this impression of him:

> We often spoke with him, sitting around a long table, in his residence on Franciszkansa Street. On weekdays the Cardinal never wore any insignia of his dignity with the exception of a Cross; he used to sit at the table in a

black cassock, his shoulders slightly hunched, attentive, listening patiently, shrewd, his face often breaking into a smile.

Those with versatile achievements to their credit often prompt the question: "How is it done?" The answer, often enough, is "on midnight oil". Versatility does, up to a point, provide its own forms of compensation, release, refreshment of spirit. One secret is certainly the ability to relax. If Bishop Wojtyla worked long hours, even fitting up a small table in his car so as to continue working while travelling from place to place, if he found the time to combine intellectual research with administrative duties, to master several languages, four entirely and two others considerably — he could also allow time for healthy recreation.

Everyone has heard that when Cardinal Wyszynski sent for him to give him the news of his nomination as a bishop he was somewhere on a canoe trip. The venue varies in different accounts from the Vistula to the Masurian lakes. Everyone has heard that while skiing in the Tatra mountains he accidentally crossed the Czechoslovak border and was arrested, first for the intrusion and then for personating the Archbishop of Krakow. He certainly liked physical exercise and allowed 300 hours a year for outdoor activities. He would camp out on excursions, saying Mass with a portable altar with two spars of wood lashed to make a cross. He was ready for long walks, went to Czestochowa several times a year on a bicycle, and if cheated of an outing by weather would revert to a game of his youth, ping-pong.

Singing seems to have come as naturally to him on such occasions as to a man who should have lived to see a Polish Pope, the great Hilaire Belloc. Like Belloc, too, he took to poetry as a relief, sending his verses to *Tygodnik Powszechny* where they appeared over the name Andrzej Jamien; even a play which he wrote has been found in dusty files and will, no doubt, give joy to many. The theme is a popular one; the wedding.

Some, but only some, instances of the banter in which he must have taken part from time to time have filtered

through the net of reverence which surrounds Popes. Once
at a clerical gathering he teased a loquacious priest with the
remark: "Your tongue will get you into Purgatory" to get
the rejoinder which he used to quote: "And there I'll have to
go through your book!" The Cardinal's work *Person and
Action* had just appeared.

Jerzy Turowicz gives an acceptable general idea of his
friend: "a modest, simple, sincere, kind man, of great good-
ness and of easy human contact". Stressing the Pope's
philosophical and theological culture, Turowicz went on:
"He is a man of great culture, in the widest sense, sensitive
to the arts and to letters, with an excellent knowledge of
modern ideological movements, open to dialogue!" He was
sensitive also to human rights. When, after a university
student, Stanislaus Pyas, was shockingly murdered in Krakow
in 1977, the Archbishop, as Wojtyla then was, supported
the Committee for the Defence of Workers, K.O.R., which
took up the incident and raised a protest.

Within seven months of Bishop Wojtyla's nomination as
Auxiliary Bishop of Krakow an event occurred which was
to have immense repercussions on the Church and to affect
especially its bishops. John XXIII called the Second Vatican
Council. Bliss it was to be alive. To be a young bishop with
intellectual interests was very heaven.

The Council made the future Pope. It served his personal
development in many ways. The Polish bishops were not
impeded in their attendance at the sessions: it would have
been difficult for the government to do so since Khruschev
allowed a Russian delegation to go to Rome, to take a place
among the Council observers. Bishop Wojtyla returned then
to the Rome of his studies and made prolonged contact
with the outside world. At a deeper level he had an opportunity to acquaint himself with the life of the universal
Church, with the day to day working of Church government
at the centre. The moment was, in his own life, appropriate.
His academic interests were still fresh. He was at an age when
he could study with interest and profit the whole changing
pastoral scene in the Church.

In particular the young Auxiliary of Krakow was not overawed by the vast assembly and all the conciliar paraphernalia. He was not cowed or bewitched by the army of experts who flocked to Rome to keep the intellectual pot simmering, if not on the boil. He was not to be patronised by any of them for he was their equal. He could face new problems without panic. If people talked to him about religious freedom he knew what tyranny was and how Nazis and communists operated. To scholarly, slightly remote talk about the People of God, laboratory language in some cases, he could oppose the experience of a nation which was actively, wholeheartedly, part of the People of God. It took a strong mind and an independent spirit to separate in those exciting times durable gains from ephemera.

The amount of documentation which began to reach the Council Fathers taxed their intellectual resources and their energy. At the outset over seventy draft texts, schemata as they were called, were considered. As the huge unwieldy body began to rationalise its procedure, plan its programme and distribute its workload, as it gained from the clash of opinions within the assembly and advice from without, more realistic estimates of what should be attempted gradually prevailed. The degree of unanimity reached in the vast majority of final votes was a feature of Vatican II which has not been fully appreciated. That, too, was bound to affect anyone with spirit and ability and love for the Church.

But there was much intellectual and emotional toil before the final votes were reached. As a member of the Polish hierarchy, Bishop Wojtyla supported a joint initiative taken by all the bishops of his country. An extensive memorandum signed by each one was submitted to the Pope asking that he, in union with the entire college of bishops, should publicly consecrate the world to the Immaculate Heart of Mary, Mother of the Church. Cardinal Wyszynski, in the name of the seventy Polish bishops, developed this idea at length in the course of the debate on the Marian Schema on 16 September 1964. He set forth the reasons and emphasised the motives. Such an act of consecration would stress the power of intercession vested in Mary, the Mother of God, and it would seek to draw this power towards us for four specific objectives: full religious liberty for all believers; respect for Christian morals and the rights of the Church; help in promoting the cause of Christian unity; peace among nations. The Cardinal pointed to the unique dignity of Mary as Mediatrix of all graces. He spoke of Poland's debt to her in the sixteenth century and in the twentieth.

The 3,500 word memorandum was composed with great care and showed solid comprehensive erudition. The greatest Polish Marian theologian of the day, Bernard Przybylski, O.P., was its principal author. The response to it did not come until the end of the third session when Paul VI proclaimed Mary Mother of the Church. Next day, he asked Cardinal Wyszynski if he was satisfied. There has been much dissatisfaction about the decline in devotion to Our Lady since Vatican II voiced in public opinion polls among Catholics. The Polish bishops are free of any blame in this regard.

Bishop Wojtyla intervened briefly on the Schema on the sources of revelation, to show the need for a precise definition of the word "source"; on the Schema on the liturgy, to plead for attention to the pastoral dimension, especially of the sacraments; and on that on social communications, to stress the importance of the moral order, the perfection of the human person, and the importance of art in a hierarchy of values.

Later, the Auxiliary Bishop of Krakow made substantial contributions to the debates on subjects known to divide the Council Fathers. The question of religious liberty was divisive. In the post-conciliar period it was to be one of Archbishop Lefebvre's grievances and he refused to sign the declaration. While the Council was still in session, sharply opposed positions were manifest. One fear was that a Council document with the title "Religious Liberty" was a blank cheque to supporters of religious indifferentism. Others thought that the Catholic Church was now sponsoring the

very liberalism which it had condemned since the French
Revolution.

Even those who wanted and worked for a Council statement on religious liberty were not agreed as to its basis.
Bishop Wojtyla spoke twice on the subject. He wanted the
text to carry conviction from its intrinsic theological content. It should not merely repeat norms already accepted
by modern states and set forth in their Constitutions or in
the declarations of international bodies:

> Instead the Council document should expound the
> Church's position on the subject. It would be more
> suitable to separate the arguments drawn from Revela-
> tion from those flowing from reason. The doctrine of
> religious liberty is contained in the very fact of Revela-
> tion. Men become more conscious of it the more they
> know theoretically and practically the dignity of the
> human person. Its meaning in social ethics presupposes
> its meaning in personal ethics. In the light of this latter
> significance, it provides a basis for dialogue between be-
> lievers and atheists. Since the Council is proclaiming the
> right of the human person to liberty in religious affairs,
> it must also insist especially on the responsibility to use
> this right. If we come to the question of limits set to the
> right of religious liberty, we have to rely on the principles
> of obedience to moral law, which is the first check on
> freedom. This freedom can be limited only when it leads
> to action malicious and against the moral law.

Here, the dignity of the human person was proposed as the
basis of the right which the Council wished to proclaim.
This solution was finally adopted. On another occasion,
Bishop Wojtyla suggested that with a view to dialogue
between the Church and the modern world, it would be
desirable to see two distinct parts in the text, even two
separate documents, one for the separated brethren, the
other for all men indiscriminately, in particular for those
with responsibility for civil order.

"From the ecumenical viewpoint", the Bishop said, "the
Declaration takes on incalculable importance." He thought,
on the other hand, that in a secular world it ought to be
possible to seek acceptance for such general principles as

these: "the human person is the end, not the instrument of social and economic order; religion is the culmination and perfection of personal life and of the aspiration to truth; freedom is needed in man's relations with God." The speaker made it quite clear that he had political rulers in mind in setting forth such ideas as an acceptable minimum in dialogue between the Church and the world.

The champions of the declaration on religious liberty within the Council were at the moment of this speech seeking allies on every side, for the hard core of opposition caused them some apprehension. Support from behind the Iron Curtain was very welcome.

Wojtyla's words on the apostolate of the laity were dictated by the experience of life behind the Iron Curtain. He was particularly happy that the obligation to the lay apostolate as taught in the Council text would be clear and compelling in places where Catholic associations (the "organised apostolate") were forbidden. The lay apostolate should be seen to stem from man's natural right to practise his convictions. He was equally insistent on the need to keep the apostolate truly Christian; it should not be used as a pretext to cover activities which have little to do with the Church.

His realism was apparent, too, in these words on dialogue between the Church and modern men: "It is not possible (for the Church) to address herself to those who are outside the Church, to those who attack her, to those who do not believe in God, in the same language as she speaks to the faithful." The audience inside St Peter's did not know that there was hard experience behind that assertion. For years, and possibly with renewed conviction after he had given public expression to this idea, Bishop Wojtyla has been a ready listener to those who have no faith. Some of them spoke of him affectionately on B.B.C. television in one of the programmes put out at the time of his election to the papacy.

Not surprisingly, then, he had a contribution to make to the debate on atheism. But just as he insisted, in speaking on religious liberty, on the obligation to seek the truth, so before treating of atheism he centred his thought on Christ's essential work of salvation, which the Church must continue:

> It is, however, necessary to emphasise even more strongly the meaning of the salvation wrought by Christ on the Cross. A pastoral concern cannot overlook the work of redemption which must be considered as a proper and constitutional element of the whole schema. Dialogue with the world cannot take as its context simply the common good and the spreading of good principles, because the Church must not renounce its own proper task, its mission of salvation.

> Undoubtedly the Church makes a contribution to the temporal good of men, but she places herself at their service above all so that they can reach their true final end, eternal salvation. Such clarity and sincerity are necessary for the successful outcome of dialogue; meanwhile in the schema the vision of the world as it should be prevails over that of the world as it is, which makes for a lack of Christian realism.

On atheism itself the speaker was equally realistic:

> From a certain standpoint the question of atheism is complementary to the Declaration on religious liberty. It would be appropriate to distinguish in the schema between atheism born of personal conviction and that which is imposed from without by pressures of every kind, physical and moral, especially when it is made impossible to profess faith in one's public or official life, one is practically compelled to profess atheism, and children's instruction is imbued with it even against the will of their parents. This offends the right of the human person, the right of the community, while it violates seriously the natural moral law. Atheism should be considered not so much as the denial of God, but as an internal state of the human person and studied according to sociological and psychological standards. The atheist is convinced of his final solitariness since, for him, God does not exist, from which comes his desire to become immortal, in a certain sense, in the collective life: whence arises the question whether collectivism favours atheism or vice versa.

These and other considerations make dialogue very difficult, especially when relativism and civic utilitarianism
are allied to atheism. If atheism is conceived as a denial
of God, dialogue must be conducted in such a way as to
show respect for the interior liberty of the person and to
show that the religious man is not entirely alienated from
the reality of the world.

Key concepts of Council teaching which would be finally
promulgated are fully manifest in Wojtyla's speeches: respect for the person and openness to be expressed in dialogue. At the outset of his episcopate, he was fortunate to
have direct, prolonged experience of the collegial aspect of
his office. For this is what the Council really meant to him:
sharing responsibility; cooperation in the affirmation of
doctrine; collective witness to the reality of the Church as a
communion receptive to the Spirit. The Popes of the Council were John XXIII, because he thought of it and called it;
Paul VI, because he saw it through its sessions; John Paul
II, because it was principally through membership of it that
he first notably acted as a bishop.

Bishop Wojtyla's presence at the third session of the
Council was saddened by the dramatically sudden death of
Bishop Joseph Gawlina. He spoke on the Marian Schema in
the assembly on 17 September, pleading for recognition of
Mary's role in Church unity. He died on the night of 19
September when at his desk preparing a speech on the
Church's care for emigrants. This was his lifework. He lies in
death under the shadow of Monte Cassino, surrounded by
the Polish soldiers, bravest of the brave, who died on its
slopes.

5 Church and State

Cardinal Wyszynski returned to Warsaw from internment "with malice towards none". He preached the doctrine of constructive patriotism. Poles had shown that they could die for the motherland; now they must show that they could live for her. His own best known publication, widely translated, is on work. He had the credentials which opened minds and hearts in his country. Imprisoned, he had rejected a compromise with the words: "Gentlemen, I shall continue to pray for you where I am." He was a symbol. High above the multitude which assembled at Jasna Gora on 26 August 1956 stood an empty chair decked with red and white roses; a token of loyalty to the great absentee, with a touch of panache.

In the heady days of liberation the government saw the Church as a steadying influence. Satisfying the liberals while not provoking the Russians into interfering was a delicate balancing act. Wyszynski helped maintain the equilibrium. There was, on the government side, a genuine conviction that Church-State relations must be handled differently. Warsaw Radio put it this way: "The return of the Primate proves that the (Stalinist) period is at an end and that we have reverted, at least in the Church-State sector, to bi-lateral discussion of controversial matters." Of course, separation of Church and State should continue, the speaker added — as if the remark were needed.

Church-State relations in Poland between 1956 and 1978 passed through three different phases: from 1956 to 1966, the year of the millennium of Christianity in Poland, an uneasy truce; from 1966 to 1970, an open clash, artificially created and with a sour aftermath; from 1971 to 1978, steady improvement with a climax of concord, just within the year preceding the election of John Paul II. The future Pope was involved in the alternating duel and dialogue from the year 1958 when he became auxiliary to Eugenius Baziak, who was acting as Administrator in the See of Krakow. At the episcopal level, Karol Wojtyla benefitted by the change of atmosphere and the new agreement between Church and State which had followed the events of 1956.

A mixed Church-State commission was set up to settle outstanding problems between the government and the episcopate. This commission removed some of the harsh disabilities afflicting the Church. The government withdrew its claim to appoint bishops, contenting itself with a form of consultation. Religious education was brought back to the schools. Religious care was guaranteed for the sick and imprisoned. The titular bishops in the western territories were accepted by the government pending their establishment as full ordinaries, that is, as bishops of legally constituted dioceses. The Holy See granted this status when a peace treaty had been concluded between Poland and Germany.

This opening spurt of goodwill lasted through the first decade of Gomulka's rule. These years included the Second Vatican Council in which the Polish bishops played their rightful part and Wojtyla emerged clearly as the brain of the episcopate. He played his part in Poland in the national programme of preparation for the millennium of Christianity in the country which the hierarchy had decreed. This was to be a nine-year novena with, in each year, an intention related to renewal of public life and morality.

During these years, the Church was not entirely free, being sporadically if not openly persecuted. State help was available for church rebuilding but grants were dilatory. Religious education was eventually denied in schools. An effort was made at Nowa Huta, as we shall see, to create something totally new in Poland: a city without a church, with no religious building of any kind. Bishop Wojtyla was directly involved in the failure of that government project, for Nowa Huta was in his diocese on the outskirts of Krakow.

Before that event, there occurred the clash of the year 1966. The anti-clerical members of the government thought that by now they could dispense with the bishops, or at least cut down their influence. They were irritated by the response from all sides to the religious millennium programme. They thought that the Church was taking the whole celebration out of their hands. For they, too, had planned ceremonies to commemorate a thousand years of Polish political existence.

To counteract the Church, the government made a sustained attack, through radio, television, and the press, on the bishops, with the Primate as the principal target. A change from 1951, however, was the fact that there was no attempt at imprisonment of bishops. Visitors to Poland would learn that the campaign was utterly unsuccessful. But it went on and on.

The pretext was the letter sent by the Polish hierarchy to the German bishops inviting them to attend the principal ceremony of the millennium, fixed for 3 May 1966. It was one of 56 such invitations which were sent from Rome where the Polish bishops were attending the final session of the Second Vatican Council. The message to the Germans recalled ancient links between the two peoples and, while recounting, as has been seen, the hard facts of the war years, offered forgiveness and urged reconciliation. The Primate gave a Christlike explanation of this gesture:

> All our messages are a response to the appeal for the greatest love, in deeds and not only in words, which Vatican II has made to the world of our time, eaten by anguish and in total disarray, offering to it thereby, the inexhaustible resources of the Church of Jesus Christ, through the power of his Gospel. Have we Polish bishops, in answering that appeal, departed from the rights conferred on us by the Holy Spirit and our mission?

He and his fellow-bishops were depicted as traitors, ready to do business with the hated enemy. His words were distorted and falsified. Editions of his books printed abroad were blocked at the frontier. A stream of hatred and misrepresentation poured out ceaselessly against him. Visas were refused to all foreign delegations wishing to attend the millennium celebrations. Among those personally refused was Pope Paul VI. The fear in government circles was that any massive international gathering inside Poland would boost the Church's prestige to a degree they could not face. There may have been some jealousy of the Polish bishops whose presence at the Council had been remarkable.

The campaign made Wyszynski a national hero. The comrades forgot that all publicity is good publicity. Led by Archbishop Wojtyla, vice-president of the national episcopal conference, the bishops rallied publicly to the Cardinal's side. They sent him an open letter signed by each member of the Polish episcopate. It said, among other things:

> Tested links of priestly love unite us with your Eminence's revered person. The fruit of that love is the unity of the Polish episcopate which pledges entire confidence to its president. Nevertheless, it is not this priestly love which prompts us to send you this letter, but rather a very lively sense of elementary, human and Christian justice. For we consider that the attacks made on you as a target, especially through press, radio and television violate this elementary, human Christian justice.

> We know well your profound attachment to our common fatherland. Your love for Poland was shown with unquestionable clarity before, during and after the war, by your thoroughly patriotic attitude toward Hitlerism and in regard to our western provinces. That is why we consider any accusation which questions your patriotism as a flagrant injustice and an outrage.

This phrase "flagrant injustice and an outrage" was repeated more than once in the denunciation of calumnies against the Cardinal. The letter stigmatised criticism of the Primate's behaviour at the Second Vatican Council and any suspicion that the other bishops were not at one with him. It deplored the use made of so-called "progressive" Catholics in the unjust campaign. The bishops expressed their gratitude for all Wyszynski had done for the Church and for the Polish people "amid so many troubles, fatigues and sufferings".

Wyszynski was not wanting in strength or nobility in face of the storm. He is granite, but granite shining in the sun. On Easter Thursday night in the Cathedral of St John the Baptist, Warsaw, he lifted the debate to the highest Christian level with words that will be recalled for ever in Poland: "You see the old men at the end of the church whose feet I will wash in the *Mandatum* ceremony. Tonight I would wash the feet of anyone, even of those who consider me their enemy."

All that the regime could do thereafter was to inject a note of meanness and pettiness into what should have been an occasion of universal joy and magnanimity. Religious assemblies and processions were planned for all the great cities. For a while Gomulka thought to challenge the Cardinal's popular appeal by timing his meetings to coincide with them. He desisted, soured. For the rest, the secret police were left to put whatever obstacles they could in the way of the Catholic processions. In Krakow, where Archbishop Wojtyla welcomed the Primate and gave him every mark of honour, these petty restrictions were applied to the point of absurdity.

Government resentment spilled over to the following year. An approach, perfectly honourable, made to General de Gaulle by the Cardinal during the French president's visit in 1967 was interpreted by the government as in some way harmful to State interests — as if Charles de Gaulle, a long-time friend of Poland, but in all things a realist who liked to know what was happening, was not thoroughly informed on the current religious position. To mark its "displeasure" the government did something very silly: it refused the Cardinal a visa to attend the Episcopal Synod in Rome in the autumn of that year. This was Church-State relations on the scale of Lilliput. The other Polish delegates, including Archbishop Wojtyla, remained in Poland as a gesture of solidarity with their Primate.

Gomulka, according to his lights and with his own strict integrity, had served his country well. He was never physically robust. The deterioration in public affairs and the economic unrest in the Baltic shipyards may have been due to his ill-health. By 1970 his course was evidently run and the search was on for a new man. Edward Gierek was chosen.

From the mid-1970s Karol Wotjyla began to emerge as a figure of great stature in the contemporary Church. During those years Church-State relations in his own country did, on the whole, improve. This was for several reasons. The fountainhead of world communism, Soviet Russia, was changing and had moved a long way from the League of Atheists and a fanatic like Yaroslavsky. Kruschev's son-in-law, editor of *Isvestia,* had visited Pope John. Podgorny, president of Russia, had an audience with Pope Paul, following in the footsteps of his Foreign Minister; so did Tito and, later, Kadar of Hungary.

Journeys in the opposite direction had been undertaken for some time by Agostino Casaroli, a papal diplomat, sometimes called the Vatican's Kissinger, instrument of the Church's dialogue with the communists.

Casaroli is a gentle, self-effacing servant of the Church. A skilful negotiator, he is too well-informed to have any illusions. He has worked in an area where risk is ubiquitous, not unlike Consalvi who bargained with Napoleon and secured a Concordat which lasted for a century, or Pacelli who negotiated with Hitler's envoy, Von Papen.

Casaroli had been on the east-European circuit since the 1960s. He had some results to show from Hungary and Jugoslavia. Poland appeared ripe for his attentions in 1974. The Vatican approach was assured at least a respectful response. Paul VI, who as a young man had been at the Warsaw Nunciature, had in the early 1970s become very popular in the country. They would still refuse him a visa to enter, they did so the Christmas before he died, for reasons which, however open to criticism, did not affect his personal image in official circles. He will be remembered

as the Pope who established normal Church authority in the
western and northern territories recovered after World War
II. Willy Brandt had, in December 1970, accepted the
Oder-Neisse line as the frontier of Poland; in the following
April the Bundestag ratified his decision. In 1972 the Pope
raised the Church jurisdictions to the status of full dioceses.
In this he was following normal procedure; for the same
reason Pius XII had refused to extend the German Concordat
to areas occupied by German forces during the war. Not
until a treaty has been signed does the Church alter existing
diocesan arrangements.

Progress depends on personalities in key positions.
Gomulka was hidebound, Gierek showed himself open to
change. He has a European background. A miner, who
was reared and who worked in France, he reputedly fought
in the Belgian Resistance during the war. He was a member
first, 1931, of the French Communist Party and later, 1937,
of the Belgian Communist Party. He returned to Poland in
1948 and was Party organiser in Upper Silesia. As Party
Secretary, from 1970, he has visited France and the United
States and welcomed Giscard d'Estaing to Poland.

Gierek's views on the religion of the Poles are very per-
tinent to negotiations between Church and State, and
between his government and the Papacy. He has been frank
on the subject. He has not said what one may surmise, that
the Warsaw government, having failed to isolate the Polish
bishops from Rome and thus reduce their power may have
changed tactics in the hope of finding post-conciliar Rome
itself more accommodating. They may have picked up ideas
about a new mentality, more openness, in the Church of
John XXIII, the Church of *Pacem in Terris* and the "spirit
of the Council". They may not have paused any more than
did others to examine the reality behind such euphoric
talk.

There is no need for guesswork here for Gierek has expressed his views quite freely in the course of interviews
given to *Newsweek,* 14 October 1974, *Le Monde,* 18 June
1975, *Der Spiegel,* 7 June 1976, and in a meeting with

workers of the communications equipment factory, PZL-Mielec, which was widely reported. The interviews are evidence of the worldwide interest in Polish Catholicism, to which Pope John Paul II referred in his letter to the faithful of his country.

To the workers Gierek said: "Relations between the Church and the People's State passed through different stages in the past. Today we can state one thing at least: there are no conflicts between the State and the Church in our country, in Poland." Gierek later stated a principle which has become basic to bridge-building between bishops and party leaders: "I believe that there is a broad field for fruitful co-operation between Church and State in the attainment of important national goals. I repeat this — I was and am for such co-operation and see great meaning in it." He was, he added, speaking for "the highest authorities in our State".

When President Giscard d'Estaing visited Poland Gierek told *Le Monde* that relations between Church and State posed no problem. He mentioned the permanent working contacts and in another remark hinted at something which would occur two years later: "I want to emphasise that we feel respect for Pope Paul VI's position on the issue of peace and the process of international *détente.*"

Gierek changed a key member of his team. Alexander Skarzynski was replaced by Kasimierz Kakol as Minister for Religious Affairs. Kakol, like Wysznyski, was at one time a journalist. The fact provided them with some off-the-cuff small talk when the Minister went to Warsaw Airport to meet the Cardinal on his return from the enthronement of John Paul II. Kakol is an economist, a lawyer who has edited a review for members of his profession, a former Professor of Journalism and Dean of the Institute of Journalism at Warsaw University. Early on, in a speech to party militants, he made a tactless remark about bishops but he has made amends for a bad start. Events have been somewhat of a strain for him. How could he know that duties moving safely within party grooves would suddenly run riot and deposit him with the president of the state and other dignitaries in St Peter's Square to witness the enthronement of a Polish Pope?

He has met, at regular intervals, Bishop Dabrowski, secretary of the National Episcopal Conference, and he received Casaroli when the Vatican diplomat visited Poland. Casaroli cannot now call on him as his duties in the Curia keep him permanently in Rome. His mantle fell on Mgr Luigi Poggi, papal representative in the working contacts with the government.

Poggi had, before the papal election, visited Poland seven times. He seems to have accepted the bishops' advice that he work in close concert with them, as he has travelled to several dioceses. He can see his opposite number in the liaison assignment in Rome, as the latter is an Embassy official, K. Szablewski.

Thus things stood in 1977, a turbulent year in Poland. Strikers had been arrested in the Radom factory and a curious protest took place: a group composed of people of very different political outlook went on hunger strike in St Martin's Church. Tension, nothing new to the Poles, rose several degrees. The situation was, however quietly defused and it was forgotten in a blaze of excitement, as two surprising news items were announced. On 29 October, Edward Gierek invited Wyszynski to a meeting in the Sejm, the parliament house: an unprecedented encounter. Next Gierek went to Rome and was received in audience by Pope Paul VI on 1 December. Speeches, which went far beyond conventional diplomacy, were exchanged. Their content marked an enormous step forward. Gierek's mother, a devout Catholic, was delighted. She saw her son on television with the Pope: another breakthrough. Her son lauded the Pope as a person, and praised his commitment to peace, in particular Casaroli's signature of the Helsinki agreement: "The position of the Holy See which supports with its high moral prestige this universal, deeply humane cause, is widely noted and fully appreciated. We see in it a lasting personal memorial to Your Holiness."

In reply Pope Paul praised Gierek's achievements in certain sectors of national life, "the initiatives which you are launching to take care of the family, your concern for the development of housing facilities for young couples, plans you have published to raise the moral standard of youth". He thought that Church and State could collaborate to their mutual advantage in the social area. Especially, the Pope underlined the Church's detachment from any political role: "The Catholic Church does not ask for privileges for itself, but only for the right to keep its identity and for the possibility of developing, without obstacles, its activities in keeping with its being and mission."

If the Pope and the Party Secretary had been asked to set the stage for the election of a Polish Pope they could hardly have done it better. There were important immediate effects of the meeting. Wyszynski, sometimes depicted by journalists as inflexible and insensitive to change, preached, on 24 December and 6 January following the papal audience, sermons which struck an immediate response in party circles. "The Church", he said on 6 January,

> does not want power. The Church does not want to create — as it is sometimes written — a state within a state . . . We do not seek to make the Church an institution of political significance. The Concordat of 1925 giving Church institutions public-legal status was in force in Poland before the war and the State was not thereby threatened in any way . . . So, there is no need to fear that if the Church secured such recognition in the contemporary setting it would abuse it, because through the past ten centuries the Church never did such a thing.

The Cardinal, with characteristic magnanimity, expressed his regret that a Catholic paper had deleted from Paul VI's address to Edward Gierek the passage which praised the positive policy and achievements of the regime.

The most important sequel to his own sermon was in an article entitled "Foundations of Co-operation and Dialogue" which appeared in the official party paper, *Polityka*. It was written by Mieczslaw F. Rakowski, who is not only editor of the paper but a member of the Central Committee of the

Polish United Workers' Party. The author welcomed what he thought was a changed outlook and made some courageous avowals and comments. "We must clear the ground", he wrote, "of prejudices, concealment, simplifications, myths, habits, the practice of seeking bad intentions in what the other party is doing. Such an approach to the problem requires from a Marxist an admission that in the past the Marxist movement as a whole was radically atheistic and declared war on the Church and religion".

He pointed to the changes in the Catholic Church: "Communists would manifest ignorance if they failed to take account of the positive changes which have already taken place in the social and political doctrine of the Roman Catholic Church". There were areas of common concern between the Church and the State "in the first place the striving to strengthen processes of *détente* and to ensure the creation of solid foundations for a lasting peace; war; or contemporary social plagues which pester vast regions of the world, such as, for instance, famine, alcoholism, drug addiction, increase in violence and brutality".

Inevitably, these comments stirred up controversy and exchange of opinions. This loosening, not to say change, of mental attitudes came at a time which was just right for Cardinal Wojtyla. He was too close to the Primate officially and personally not to have followed the course of events and the emergence of new ideas very attentively.

Church-State relations in Poland still remain enigmatic, unique. Wyszynski always tells his brother bishops and others who fear that one day they might have similar problems in their own countries, that the Polish methods might not help them. He does not say what many think: you cannot easily find a Wyszyanski.

6 Cardinal

The Archbishop of Krakow was named Cardinal by Pope
Paul VI on 26 June 1967; the honour has been traditional
in the See of Krakow. Cardinal Pericle Felici, well known to
Wojtyla as Secretary General of the Council, was promoted
the same day; he would announce the election of John Paul
II to the crowd in St Peter's Square on 16 October 1978.

The College of Cardinals is close to the Pope in Church
affairs if not actual government. The Cardinals serve on
the governing bodies of the Vatican ministries, generally
styled Congregations. Cardinal Wojtyla was a member of
three, for Priests, for Divine Worship and for Catholic
Education. He was also consultant to the Papal Council for
the Lay Apostolate. Since 1969 he has been a member of the
fifteen strong Council of the General Secretariat of the
Episcopal Synod. It is said that he was offered the presi-
dency of the International Commission for Justice and Peace,
but declined as it would mean excessive absence from his
diocese.

The Polish Church is generally well represented in the
Roman Curia. Two prelates with whom Cardinal Wojtyla
had ties of close friendship have recently occupied important posts in the Vatican administration: Bishop Ladislaus
Rubin, Secretary General of the Episcopal Synod, and
Archbishop Andrzej Maria Deskur, president of the Papal
Commission for Social Communications. The latter was, at
the time of his episcopal ordination, received with special
honour at Krakow by Cardinal Wojtyla, who asked publicly
for prayers on Deskur's behalf. During the conclave he suffered a grave heart attack. To see him in a Roman hospital

63

John Paul II made his first journey outside Vatican City.

Another Polish prelate with a record of long service in the Curia, Cardinal Filipiak, formerly Dean of the Roman Rota, died in Poznan, where he lived in retirement, some days before the conclave.

When Cardinal Wojtyla travelled to Rome to fulfil the various new duties now incumbent on him he would meet these or some of his other fellow-countrymen working in Italy, especially in Vatican City. He did not attend the first meeting of the Episcopal Synod in 1967, but was at every subsequent meeting. He had increased responsibility as a member of the Synod Council. He took an active part in the deliberations and attracted particular attention during two meetings, in 1971 and 1974.

A principal theme of the 1971 Synod was the priesthood. During the session, on 17 October, Maximilian Kolbe, was beatified. He starved to death in Auschwitz concentration camp after freely offering to take the place of a young married man condemned to death. The camp was in the diocese of Krakow so the Cardinal gave a press conference in French in Vatican City to explain the event. "Next Sunday," he said,

> the Beatification will take place of one whose life and death have particular relevance to the world of our time. Maximilian Kolbe, a Franciscan religious, has aroused world-wide interest by the sacrifice which he freely chose and accepted with love, on behalf of someone unknown, the father of a family, who had been marked out to die of hunger and of thirst with nine other convicts, as reprisals for an escapee. This man, named Gajowniczek, is in Rome and he will be present at the glorification of the one thanks to whom he survived the hell of the concentration camp. It is now thirty years since the day, the Vigil of the Assumption, 1941, when Fr Maximilian Kilbe, sole survivor of the condemned group, was liquidated by a phenol injection. His body went with millions of others, to one of the crematoria which burned day and night at Auschwitz. Thus was fulfilled the wish which he had so often expressed; "I would want my ashes scattered to the four points of the horizon." Little did he think that his desire

would be realised to the letter, but that far from disappearing without trace his humble wish would attract the attention of the universal Church. Rarely has their been such unanimity in a judgement on holiness.

Immediately arises a question which is put more and more insistently: *"Why* Fr Maximilian Kolbe?" Have other convicts not given the witness of heroic brotherly love in the death camps, for example the Polish bishop Mgr Kozal who literally faced death by starvation as he distributed his meagre food rations among his fellow internees? As the Church which reads the "signs of the times" gives us this priest as our model, what is it saying to us?

For note carefully that this forty-seven-year-old man who with exemplary fidelity had realised the ideal of St Francis, wanted to die as a *priest*. When "Bloody Fritch", absolutely stunned by the boldness of a convict who wanted to take the place of a condemned man, put him this brutal question: "Who are you anyway?" Maximilian Kolbe gave this simple answer: "A Catholic priest."

It was then as a priest that he accompanied the unfortunate flock of nine men condemned to death. He was not content to have saved the tenth; he must now help the nine others to die. From the moment that the fateful door closed on the condemned group he took charge of all of them, not them only but others who were dying of starvation in the nearby bunkers, whose howling as of wild beasts caused everyone who came near them to shudder . . . In fact from the moment that Fr Kolbe was in their midst these unfortunate people suddenly felt that they were protected and helped and the cells wherein they awaited the inexorable climax resounded with prayers and hymns, The jailers themselves were overwhelmed by the whole thing: "So was haben wir nie gesehen", they said. We shall now know until the "Day of the Lord" whether there were "good thieves" among them converted, if only at the last moment, by this heroic witness. The fact remains, and all the survivors of Auschwitz know it well, that from the Assumption of 1941 the camp became less of a hell.

At an hour when many priests throughout the world question themselves on their "identity", Fr Maximilian Kolbe rises in our midst to give the answer not in theological speeches, but in his life and his death.

The Cardinal then emphasised the totally Christlike idealism of the Franciscan *beatus*. He outlined his virtuous character, displayed especially in his spirit of total forgiveness in
the Pawiak prison in Warsaw and later in Auschwitz: "He
broke the infernal cycle of hatred."

Krakow was a place beloved in life by Fr Kolbe. Now its
archbishop sketched very briefly the Franciscan priest's
astonishing apostolate, his ambition, even in the 1930s, to
use every modern means to serve the gospel; his missionary
life in Japan; Niepokalanow outside Warsaw, his greatest
monument, where 700 Franciscans worked for the glory of
God; his Marian spirituality; his Marian theology which,
as the Cardinal said, so closely resembles that of Vatican II.

The theme of the 1974 Synod was evangelisation in the
world today, which was also linked with Vatican II and
certainly not alien to the life of Fr Kolbe. After the Council,
some confusion of thought, some error, some controversy,
some unresolved questions had come to the surface on
themes which are at the very heart of the Church's existence: the relationship between evangelisation and development; the meaning of "liberation", an idea particularly
dear to Latin American theologians; the new perspectives
opened by the Council declaration on the non-Christian
religions. The report prepared by Cardinal Wojtyla on
the theological part of the Synod theme was one of the
principal documents which the Synod submitted to Pope
Paul to help him in writing his encyclical on evangelisation:
Evangelii Nuntiandi. The composition of this text was the
most important task thus far entrusted to the Archbishop
of Krakow. To his sucess in the task may perhaps be due
the decision taken by Pope Paul two years later to invite
him to preach the Lenten retreat to the papal household
in St Mathilda's chapel. The retreat lectures, delivered in
Italian and published in book form shortly after, *Sign of
Contradiction*, are now, like all Karol Wojtyla's writings,
widely translated and a favourite quarry for the antholo-
gists. That it should be thus widely quoted is understandable as it gives, in lively compelling form, the practical out-

look of this man on the Christian message. It is his spiritual doctrine nourished by learning and tested by experience, an informed personal statement of Christian values. Another dimension of this outlook is apparent in the author's contribution, on catechesis dealing with Our Lady and the saints, to the 1977 Episcopal Synod.

The mind of Karol Wojtyla would merit extended analysis and evaluation. Already, three years before his election to the Papacy, a student at the Angelico, Fr Jan Piatek, had presented to the Faculty of Philosophy an academic dissertation entitled "Person and Love in the philosophical thought of Cardinal Karol Wojtyla". In 1974, a specialist review, *Rivista di Teologia Morale,* noted Wojtyla's important research and reflection not only on Max Scheler but on "faith and humanism, the evangelical principle of imitation, natural law" commending especially his exceptionally rigorous method.

Wojtyla in his fifties was cut off from the academic world, immersed in administration and pastoral work. Yet, without the stimulus of the university world his intellectual power increased and his literary production was quite substantial. As well as theological papers and homilies which had to have some body, he brought out a book on personal love and sexuality and three other works, one of which was *Sign of Contradiction.*

In the Council, Bishop Wojtyla had given particular attention to marriage problems, serving on a commission on the subject. He was named a member of the papal commission on population, the family and births. This was the advisory body so much discussed at the time of Pope Paul's encyclical *Humanae Vitae.* "Why," it has been asked about Cardinal Wojtyla, "was he absent from the 1966 meeting of the commission, the final one when a vote was taken?" "How would he have voted?" The history of the millennium year, already outlined, will answer the first question: every Polish bishop felt it a duty to remain in the country to show solidarity with the Primate.

The book, *Love and Responsibility,* which first appeared

in 1960 and has been re-edited, as well as being translated into French and Italian, will give some answer to the second question. The book is not, however, a defence of *Humanae Vitae*, for it appeared six years before the encyclical. It is, rather, a book which seeks to enlighten modern theories of sexuality with Christian idealism, with the personalist philosophy which is the core of the author's thinking. Cardinal Suenens approached the problem from a different viewpoint in his book *Love and Self-Control,* but not in the comprehensive manner of Wojtyla's work.

The key sentence to the whole work is probably this: "The essence of love is most profoundly realised in the gift of self which the loving person makes to the person loved." The book was written before Vatican II but the author dealt in a satisfying way with a problem which came to a head during the Council in the theological debates on marriage and which had been raised in the schools during the preceding decades: "What is the relationship between the 'ends of matrimony', between the mutual love of the partners and the begetting of children?" "The idea that the ends of marriage could be attained without the support of the personalist norm would be profoundly anti-Christian, for it would be contrary to the essential moral principle of the Gospel. That is why one must carefully avoid a superficial interpretation of the Church's teaching on the ends of marriage."

The book deals in a dignified way with sexual differences; different levels of experience; the relationship between knowing and loving in the inter-personal human context; the role of education, psychotherapy and medical sexology; and even — with delicacy but realism — the physiological aspect of marital love.

In 1969, Cardinal Wojtyla published *Person and Action,* sponsored by the Polish Theological Society in Krakow. In a paper read to the International Congress for the seventh centenary of St Thomas Aquinas in Rome in 1974, he explained his purpose in writing the book and the effect it had in Polish academic circles. He felt that there was "an

urgent need for a confrontation of the metaphysical con-
ceptions of the person which we find in St Thomas and the
tradition of Thomism with the total human experience".
The Cardinal summarised reactions to the book as follows:

> The discussion begun during the meeting of philosophers
> at the Catholic University of Lublin in 1970 was continued
> in various written comments and articles, some twenty
> in all, which are to be published in the 1973 volume of
> the annual *Analecta Cracovensia.* Taking part in the dis-
> cussion were representatives of various Catholic centres
> of learning, primarily those of Lublin, Warsaw and
> Krakow; each of them concentrated on a somewhat dif-
> ferent line of philosophy . . . *Person and Action* has also
> attracted the attention of some Marxist philosophers
> who, though they did not take part in the meeting at
> Lublin or in the subsequent discussion, have published
> their opinions on the book.

Before the papal election this work on the human person
was being translated by his fellow-Pole, Anna-Teresa
Tymieniecka, who heads the Institute for Advanced Phe-
nomenological Research in Boston, She summarised
Wojtyla's thought thus: "He stresses the irreducible value
of the human person. He finds a spiritual dimension in
human conception of society." In stressing the dignity
and claims of the person, Wojtyla was in harmony with a
persistent theme in recent papal and Council teaching.
This is the surest anchor-plate in face of the harsh creed
of the tyrants and the weak drift of the permissives.

In 1972 the Cardinal published a work of theological
import, *Foundations of Renewal, A treatise on the im-
plementation of Vatican II.* It runs to 366 pages and may
be the most important work on Council teaching by a
bishop who helped to shape it. We have had many studies
by the experts who worked in the back rooms but few
Council Fathers have composed comprehensive close-knit
treatises of this size. The author wished to help people
understand Council documents and to guide the reader in
the use of them. He wished to answer in terms of Council
teaching such questions as "Church, what sayest thou of

thyself? What is the significance of having the faith, of being a Catholic, a member of the Church?" He has pithy statements like, "For we are the Church and at the same time we believe in the Church", but in the judgement of a Polish Jesuit commentator the book is not easy reading. However, it remains a substantial work on a capital event in Church history and theology by a bishop who has become Pope.

The future Pope was encouraging to intellectuals in a personal way. On 20 April 1978 a symposium was held in the episcopal residence in Krakow on "Contemporary Philosophy and the future of Metaphysics". Papers were read by W. Strotewski, Associate Professor of the Jagiellonian University on "Transcendentalia and Values", by Rev. M. Jaworski, Dean of the Theological Faculty of Krakow University on "The Problem of identity and Metaphysics", by Dr K. Tarnowski of Krakow University on "Heidegger and the future of Metaphysics" and by Rev. J. Tischner of Krakow Seminary on "Thinking in the light of Metaphysics". This was not the "flying university", whose clandestine lectures were much frowned on by the regime, which could not control or even check their content, but it must have heartened the academics taking part.

Fully installed as Cardinal with heavy commitments on every side at home and abroad, Wojtyla kept up his programme of open house. He rose at 5.30, said Mass in the dining-room which is quite near the kitchen, and then retired to work and pray, sometimes working in the oratory. He was not to be disturbed before eleven o'clock. Then, until lunch, he was available to all who called. Well-known visitors like Bishop Hnilica have described the queues waiting to be received by the Cardinal. There was an arrangement that the poor would be received and helped in a special room.

Groups of intellectuals, writers, artists, professional people, were so constantly meeting the Cardinal that the sisters, after his departure, before the arrival of his successor, found the whole building unbearably empty. One felt

walking through it that a great presence had been with-
drawn. Symbolic of this was the empty space in the oratory
left by the image of Our Lady of Czestochowa, given to the
Cardinal by Wyszynski.

Meetings of greater import, especially and officially fostered by the Cardinal, were held annually to prepare the
diocesan Synod which would coincide with the ninth centenary of St Stanislaus in 1979. Priests and laity were
represented, and every year progress was reported on
sectional meetings.

We must turn now to Nowa Huta, symbol of a pastoral
problem crucial in the time of Cardinal Wojtyla. Photographs of the huge modernistic church have been carried by
Time and *Newsweek* magazines in their excellent cover
stories on the new Pope. Nowa Huta was planned as a
socialist answer to Christian Krakow. It would rise as a
vast, drab suburb, providing the labour-force for the
Lenin Steelworks, the largest in Europe. The industrial
complex has 35,000 employees mostly drawn from the
countryside, uprooted, vulnerable, it might have appeared,
to plausible anti-religious propaganda. The urban settle-
ment was to be godless as are the vast new residential quarters that have been added to the city of Moscow. Everything would be provided, every service available, except
religion. Nowa Huta would be the first town in Polish
history without a church.

That was not how the inhabitants of Nowa Huta saw
things. Let Cardinal Wojtyla narrate and explain what
happened. Let him be the spokesman of the faithful of
Nowa Huta. A year before he officiated at the blessing of
the church he preached a memorable sermon in the presence
of the Vatican representative, Mgr Luigi Poggi.

Your Excellency, the church where we meet today was
born of great, of atrocious, suffering. The suffering from
which the church at Nowa Huta, named for the Mother
of God, Queen of Poland, was born, is of great historical
moment. For they wanted to build a new city, Nowa
Huta, a new Krakow, as a town without God and without

Church, at least without a new church. Then the people who came here from widely different regions of Poland made it quite clear that they did not want to build the new city of Nowa Huta without a new church. The fact is extremely eloquent. It was so some decades ago when the decisive events about Nowa Huta were taking place. It is still so today.

Let me explain the eloquence of this fact right to the end. This is what was said aloud at the time by the Polish people: "You cannot fight against religion in the name of the working class. You cannot take advantage of workers in the struggle against religion. For the Polish working class wants religion and constantly sings: 'We want God'." How often have we sung that beneath the cross raised on the plot where the church was to be built, and here on the new site and at Mistrezejowice, on the Wzgorza, at Osiedle Padwawelskie and in so many other places? Who else but the Polish worker sings "We want God"? Who else builds churches? Who patiently keeps sending delegations to the authorities that churches may be built?

In Poland you cannot struggle against religion in the name of the workers, because for the Polish worker religion is wealth, light, way, truth and life . . . Man cannot live fully if his gaze is not on God, if he is denied the possibility of saying "We want God" and accomplishing what he means by it. For this reason we must affirm quite clearly that the struggle against religion, against God, is a struggle against man. It leads to a condition in which men who sing "We want God", who believe in God and love him are victims of discrimination because of their faith. Is that a good thing? Is that justice? There cannot be a just society where the laws of man's spiritual life are not entirely and at all times respected. These laws can be summarised in the right to religious liberty and freedom of conscience.

The Cardinal stressed the identity of purpose that existed between the teaching of the Popes, of the Council and of the Synods, particularly of the most recent one, and the work of the Polish bishops on behalf of their people. "Our work, our episcopal ministry in the Church is one with the pastoral concern of the Holy Father." This was defence of religious liberty in a down-to-earth situation somewhat different from the Council assembly in St Peter's. It was an object lesson in the harsh realities of co-existence to Mgr Poggi and his spiritual leader in Rome.

For the story of Nowa Huta justified the epithet used by Wojtyla, "atrocious". The thousands who met for Mass in a little wooden chapel in the nearby countryside sent numerous petitions to the authorities for permission to build a church. In the 1956 "thaw" permission was finally given, a site allocated and a large wooden cross erected there. The architect for the new church was Wojciech Pietrzyk and his design, an oval building resembling an ark crowned with a steel mast in the shape of a cross, was symbolic. Having got permission and a site, the people then found that local officials with control of building materials, machinery and electric power were blocking further progress of any kind.

The people's frustration soon turned to rage. The site, they learned, would be used for a school and the cross taken down. The attempt to remove it provoked a riot. The police arrived, set dogs on the crowd and beat the people harshly with truncheons. Next, workers left the factories and joined in the defence of the cross. The police brought up fire hoses which they used along with tear gas to disperse the infuriated people. The government yielded. On 13 October 1967, permission to build was once more given.

Construction took ten years, during which time the faithful of Nowa Huta heard Mass around an altar placed on the roof of a convent. The open-air celebration was attended winter and summer by huge crowds. Factory workers came after hours to work without pay on the building for which the petty officials would not give an adequate work-force. When the steel roof supports had to be welded electric current was cut off until five in the afternoon. No cranes were allowed on the site until foreign currency was subscribed. Cement mixers were withheld so all the cement was mixed by hand and carried in wheelbarrows.

Meanwhile, an immense movement of goodwill was generated, reminiscent of the corporate efforts which built

the medieval cathedrals. Students came from all over Poland
during holiday time. Youth groups, members of the German
Reconciliation Movement, came to Poland to practise their
motto, "Action is a sign of Penance". Work always began
on the site with architect, engineer, all engaged in the task,
joining in prayer. Despite every kind of delaying tactics,
the church was ready for consecration in May 1977. It was
a day of grace for pastor and people, part of the Polish
miracle. The stark gigantic crucifix in the middle of the
church, the concentration camp Pietàs by Antoniego Kzasy,
spoke of victory.

That day the crowd was over 50,000. All Polish dioceses
and Catholic groups were represented. There were pilgrims
from Austria with gifts, a Dutch group who had offered
bells to the church, delegations from France, Belgium,
Portugal and other countries. There were many telegrams of
congratulation, including one from the Primate and from
Paul VI. The Pope had taken a special interest in the
church. He had sent stone from St Peter's Tomb to be
placed in the foundations and some of the lunar rock which
the American astronauts had presented to him. He donated
the Carrara marble altar.

The event was enthusiastically covered in the Catholic
press. Still more significant is the history of Catholic practice in the church ever since. The church of the largest parish
in Poland is one of the best attended in the world. On Sun-
days, Masses begin before dawn and go on all day on the
hour. The building, of which the nave alone can hold 5,000
people, is crowded to the door, with overflowing attendance
sometimes twenty deep. An estimated 10,000 attend each
Mass. In May 1975, 1,600 children received their first Holy
Communion there. One may very well accept the judgement of a commentator that this parish is "without equal
in Europe and in the world". The whole spiritual phenomenon reminds one of the crowds reported in certain missionary lands, like Iboland in Nigeria, where you will also
find the same large numbers of seminarists.

The Church in Poland is oriented to the future and supported by the past. Religious anniversaries are enthusiastically celebrated. Cardinal Wojtyla had already set elaborate preparations under way for the nine hundredth anniversary, in 1979, of the martyrdom of St Stanislaus. Four years ago, the Cardinal received a papal letter encouraging the commemoration of the six hundredth anniversary of the birth of a saintly Polish Queen, Hedwiga. This is not the saint on whose feastday John Paul II was elected, but she is venerated as a saint who, it is hoped, will one day be so recognised by the Church. Queen Hedwiga was especially noted for works of charity and for founding the theological faculty of the Jagiellonian University of Krakow.

About the same time, on 16 May 1975, the Cardinal presided at ceremonies commemorating the hundred and fiftieth anniversary of the birth of Mother Angela Truszkowska, foundress of the Felician Sisters. This Polish congregation is dedicated to works of charity and education. It numbers over 3,400 members in ninety-three communities in Poland, and it has 360 other communities throughout the world. Mother Angela died and is buried in Krakow. The cause of her beatification was introduced in Rome in 1959.

Another Polish foundation centred in Krakow held its twelfth general chapter in June 1976. The Congregation of St Michael the Archangel was founded in 1897 by Fr Bronislaw Markiewicz to help lonely, abandoned children. The Higher Institute of Catechetics was honoured that year too. The first of its kind in the world, it was founded by Cardinal Sapieha in 1950. It is run in Krakow by the Ursuline Sisters, whose centenary in the city was commemorated. Ceremonies of this kind become an unending chain in the life of a churchman so talented, so fluent in several languages as was Cardinal Wojtyla.

The members of the Polish diaspora, some ten million people widely scattered around the world, are especially numerous in North America. So, when Cardinal Wojtyla attended the Eucharistic Congresses at Melbourne in 1973 and Philadelphia in 1976, he went on to visit Polish groups

in New Zealand and throughout the United States and
Canada. He reported back to the meeting of the Polish
national episcopal conference on all occasions. Polish
bishops maintain strong links with the emigrants. There
were, also, occasions like the symposium of European
Bishops held in Rome in October 1975 attended by a Polish
delegation led by Cardinal Wojtyla. At a plenary session he
read a paper entitled "The Bishop, servant of the faith".

All the invitations to speak were not from abroad. As
Vice-President of the national episcopal conference the
Cardinal was expected to fill a heavy round of speaking
engagements in various centres of Polish Catholic life. He
was host in September 1976 to the third congress of Polish
theologians which was held in Krakow, attended by 700
professors and lecturers from universities and senior seminaries. The subject of this meeting, which was proclaimed
"one of the major intellectual events" in the history of
Polish theology, was "Theology — Science of God".
The first and second congresses, held in Lublin in 1966
and 1971, had dealt with the "Theology of the Council"
and "Theology and Anthropology" respectively. The Cardinal urged the congress to face the task which had been
set by the second Lublin meeting, analysis of a distinctive
Polish theology.

Earlier that year, he had presided over the meeting of
the episcopal commission for the Lay Apostolate held also
in Krakow, the theme being education for dialogue in the
Church. The next year, 1977, he read a paper entitled
"The basic problem in conducting the ministry and preaching programme for 1977-78 — man in the Church community — responsibility for the Church", to a national
gathering of diocesan directors of ministry.

The Cardinal's programme of work in 1978 prior to his
election as Pope has been closely scrutinised for signs of
things to come. He travelled twice to Italy on official duties.
He preached an important sermon on Christian unity in
the Dominican church in Krakow at the end of the Octave
of Prayer. Evangelist Billy Graham was preaching to a crow-

ded audience in St Anne's Church in Krakow four days before the election of John Paul II, at his invitation. In September, the future Pope was the guest of the German bishops at the annual meeting of the episcopal conference at Fulda and went on with Wyszynski to Dachau: this was the public seal on German-Polish reconciliation in the spirit of Christ.

The Cardinal was chosen to address the giant assembly at Piekary in May. He spoke of the rights of the workers, of the need for leisure, and made a plea to the authorities for the time on radio or television for broadcasting Mass to the sick and aged. In June, he was in Milan, one of the two main speakers at the conference held for the tenth anniversary of *Humanae Vitae*. The other was Fr G. Martalet, S.J., who is thought to have worked on the draft of the encyclical. The text of Cardinal Wojtyla's lecture "Love and Responsibility", a personalist, idealistic doctrine of conjugal love, is widely diffused. For the paper, the author drew on his book, *Love and Responsibility,* on the *Introduction to Humanae Vitae* which he published in 1969, on the pastoral issued by the bishops in that year, on which he certainly worked, as well as on a lecture he gave in 1976 to the Family Institute in Krakow. The Milan meeting was attended by 350 representatives from fifty-seven countries, including thirty-seven Third World countries.

There was something appropriate in the appearance of a Polish prelate at testing intellectual encounters. For the Catholic Church in Poland, which must have the highest degree of religious attendance in the world, is also enjoying an intellectual renaissance. Symbols of this advance are, among many others, the massive history of Polish theology currently appearing under the aegis of Lublin University and, under the same sponsorship, the twelve volume, *Encyklopedia Katolicka,* planned to appear over the period 1973-1993.

An editorial board works with 45 specialists responsible for different sections, a technical editorial group of eighteen, and 500 contributors from Poland and abroad.

The work aims at total scientific precision, with emphasis on dialogue; positive presentation, rather than controversy; a general ecumenical interest; and openness to contributions from outside the Catholic communion when these would enlighten. The article, "Bishop", for example, is dealt with by Anglican, Orthodox, Lutheran, Old Catholic as well as Catholic contributors. The choice of subjects is wide, with theology the overall preoccupation, but remote intellectualism is avoided.

7 Pope

It will be for Pope Paul VI's biographer to show how he prepared the way for a non-Italian Pope. He so enlarged the College of Cardinals that such a choice could be easily made. In the conclaves after his death there were only 26 Italians in a voting body of 111. He had also, as the opportunity occurred, appointed non-Italians as heads of the various Vatican ministries or Congregations: Villot, a Frenchman, Secretary of State and Camerlengo of the Holy Roman Church with a number of other exalted Curial titles; Seper, a Jugoslav, Prefect of the Congregation for the Doctrine of the Faith, watchdog of orthodoxy; Knox, an Australian, head of the Congregation responsible for the Liturgy and the Discipline of the Sacraments: Garrone, a Frenchman, Prefect of the Congregation for Catholic Education; Rossi, a Brazilian, directing the Congregation for the Evangelisation of Peoples, the old Congregation for the Propagation of the Faith; Wright, an American, head of the Congregation for Priests. Non-Italians, Willebrands, Koenig, Roy, are found in the highest posts of the secretariats, councils and commissions set up after Vatican II. One has to scan the list to find an Italian, someone like Pignedoli, president of the Secretariat for Non-Christians.

The immediate close collaborators of Paul VI's successor would then be an international company. The Pope strove to achieve unity, to hold the balance between the disruptive movements within the Church on the right and on the left. It is still too early to say that he saw the Catholic body through the post-conciliar crisis. He worked for consensus among Catholics, consensus tolerant of pluralism within

just limits. The International Theological Commission
which he established was broadly based. He widened the
Biblical Commission, once a synonym for intransigence,
to include scholars versed in modern methods. He opened
the Vatican Archives for the period of World War II.

The consensus which the Pope sought was reflected in
the successive sessions of the Episcopal Synod, which itself
was his creation. These lacked the tension coming from rival
groups which had been food and drink to the journalists
reporting on the Council. The two conclaves which met
in August and September 1978 had the advantage of this
previous experience, for a number of the Cardinals had
been Synod members. When Pope Paul died, Cardinal
Villot, Camerlengo, had the happy idea of stretching the
time allowed before the conclave met to the limit allowed
by Church law. Since the Cardinals as an interim governing
body of the Church met each day they had time to know
each other well; those excluded from the conclave by the
age limit were brought into the deliberations, a delicate
touch. The voters kept their thoughts to themselves, but
that they had thoughts before meeting in conclave seemed
clear from the swiftness of the result: Cardinal Luciani, unknown to all, even the experts, as a serious candidate, was
chosen in one day.

As things were to work out later it was reassuring that an
Italian was elected in the first conclave. This showed that
intrinsic merit would be the determining factor. On a lower
level it was also preferable that any changes in the ritual of
enthronement would be made by an Italian Pope; such
changes made by a foreigner could have looked abrupt and
disrespectful. John Paul I simplified the ritual and John
Paul II followed suit.

After the election of John Paul I the two Polish Cardinals
sent to the faithful of their country the following statement:

On the feast of Our Lady of Czestochowa, Saturday, 26
August, a new successor to St Peter was elected by the
conclave of 111 cardinals representing the Catholic
Church from all five continents. He was Cardinal Albino

Luciani, Patriarch of Venice who took the name of John Paul I. The election of the Pope in one day is a visible sign of Divine Providence. It revealed the "gift of unity in the Holy Spirit" for which the Church prayed at the beginning of the Mass. It revealed in particular the mediation of the Mother of the Church who on that day led the thoughts and hearts of the cardinals, helping them to elect the man so much awaited by the Church.

For us Poles the choice of John Paul I will always be linked with the feast of Our Lady of Czestochowa. In the Czestochowa monastery we prayed for a Pastor in the See of Peter pleasing to the heart of God. Through Our Lady we shall commend the pontificate to God's care, asking for his blessing upon it and for the grace of enduring peace. Every evening we shall pray at the Mass said at Jasna Gora for the intentions of John Paul I, that he may have the assistance of the Mother of the Church.

We send you the blessing of the Holy Father John Paul I.

Cardinal Wojtyla returned from the conclave via Turin, where he went to see the Holy Shroud, which was displayed in public for six weeks from late August to early October. He brought with him to the episcopal residence in Franciszkansa Street a photograph of John Paul I; it hangs in one of the large reception rooms near the lifesize portrait of St Pius X, Sapieha's hero. Did the Cardinal have any idea that he would shortly succeed them in the high office? The sisters remember that when he was told that John Paul I had died he murmured "Gesu Maria" and, as if speaking to himself, added: "What will happen now?"

Bishop Hnilica who happened to be on the same plane as the two Polish Cardinals when they were travelling to Rome for Pope Paul's funeral said to them: "Your Eminences, it is my most fervant wish that one of you will not return to Poland, but will remain in Rome." "Not one only," replied Cardinal Wojtyla. "Either both or none." "Yes," continued the Czech bishop, "one as Pope and the other as Secretary of State".

Did the Cardinals entering the second conclave have any idea that they would elect the young Polish Cardinal? Most commentators think that the issue was between Cardinal

Siri, Archbishop of Genoa, and Cardinal Benelli, Archbishop of Florence. Siri is a conservative, a man of great integrity, totally dedicated to the Church. Benelli was Paul VI's right-hand man until a short time before the Pope's death when he was appointed to the See of Florence and named Cardinal. He had been the power behind the throne, though subordinate in office to the French Secretary of State.

A prelate with long, high-level experience of the Curia who has served abroad is automatically thought of for the highest office. The names of other Italian Cardinals were bandied about and may have been considered. We do not know what took place inside the conclave. Some of the conjecture has been based on voting estimates before it started; possibly individual Cardinals stated their intention. But even here there is a margin of error: they may have changed when the voting began. To the certain knowledge of the present writer, five Cardinals who agreed at a recent conclave that they would not vote for a particular candidate, all changed their minds separately the following morning and supported him. It is said that when, in the last election, the two foremost Italian candidates were deadlocked with no hope of a break, the Germans and Koenig launched Wojtyla's name. He was well known to all; he had accompanied Wyszynski to the meeting of the German episcopal conference in September. But again, that is hearsay at a considerable remove.

The bold, imaginative stroke of electing a young Cardinal from a country within the communist hegemony astonished the world. But mingled with the astonishment there was almost everywhere ungrudging admiration. The admiration passed quickly from the conclave to the man, as his fascinating lifestory became known and as his conduct of the papal office was seen. For months the Catholic Church, the Papacy in particular, has been at the centre of world curiosity. The media have been sated with what they live on, the unusual, the exceptional. Television could scarcely look for a more appropriate setting for open-air religious events than St Peter's Square: what a backdrop Michelangelo created,

what a setting Bernini added to it. Rarely has television had
in rapid succession such colourful spectacles as sprang up
around the Pope in Latin America.

A number of formal meetings with notabilities or delegations followed the enthronement of the Pope. Already in
those early days John Paul II's distinctive personality and
his ability to enunciate telling truth were manifest. To journalists the man who had himself contributed from time to
time to *Tygodnik Powszechny* spoke these comforting words.

> It is my precise wish that the purveyors of religious in-
> formation will always receive the help they need from
> the competent ecclesiastical authorities. The latter should
> welcome them with respect for their conviction and their
> profession, provide them with very adequate, very objec-
> tive documentation, but also put before them the Chris-
> tian perspective wherein facts take on their true meaning
> for the Church and mankind.

The Pope from behind the Iron Curtain had this to say
to the diplomats accredited to the Holy See — knowing
that his words would not be lost on governments which
do not have such representation:

> The Church, on the other hand, and the Holy See in
> particular, asks your nations, your governments to give
> increasing consideration to a certain number of needs.
> The Holy See does not seek this for itself. It does so,
> in union with the local episcopate so that Christians and
> believers who live in your countries, without any particu-
> lar privilege but in full justice, may be able to nourish
> their faith, ensure religious worship and be admitted as
> loyal citizens to a full share in social life. The Holy See
> does this equally in the interest of all men whoever they
> may be, knowing that liberty, respect for the life and
> dignity of persons — who are never mere instruments —
> equity in remuneration, professional conscientiousness
> in work and joint pursuit of the common good, the spirit
> of reconciliation, openness to spiritual values are all fun-
> damental requirements of harmonious social life, of the
> progress of citizens and of their civilisation.

Incessantly acclaimed by crowds in St Peter's, John Paul
II has appealed particularly to young people, as he did
formerly in Krakow. His oratorial gift has been compared to

that of Pius XII. More impressive still is the content of his pronouncements. Though not precipitate he has not been afraid to grasp the nettle where need be: witness his out-right condemnation of abortion, repeated despite the clamour raised in certain quarters and the allegation that he was interfering in Italian politics.

He has gone straight to the heart of the Church's crisis. Take Latin America. For years that continent has been in a ferment: with clashing ideologies; raw tyranny; theologians trying to fit politics and religion into some kind of impossible amalgam; the cries of the oppressed, the hungry, the illiterate and the diseased; the rebuke implicit in events themselves to certain prelates who are too close to the political establish-ment; the losses in clerical personnel through despair, de-featism or just lethargy in face of apparently impossible tasks.

To co-ordinate programmes designed to meet these urgent needs in an area which contains one third of the Church's membership Pius XII, in 1955, established the Latin American Episcopal Council. It is a model of Church organisation on a continental scale. Paul VI attended the last meeting of the general assembly at Medellin in 1968. John Paul II has said that the conclusions then reached con-tained positive elements, but he also noted that there had been "incorrect interpretations which called for calm dis-cernment, opportune criticism and clear choices of position".

The general assembly of 1979 which was convoked by Paul VI was to reflect, at Puebla, on all this tangle of theories and policies, and plot the course ahead. It would have been easy for John Paul II to plead newness to his office as an excuse for absence. He went and delivered a magisterial pronouncement which may mark a decisive moment of clarity in the seething debates and questionings. In a characteristic passage he spoke to the advocates of a Christ "adapted" to the revolutionary needs of the con-tinent: "Any form of silence, disregard, mutilation or in-adequate emphasis which, in regard to the whole mystery of Christ, diverges from the Church's faith cannot be a valid content of evangelisation."

Those who in their enthusiasm for liberation theology would compromise on the transcendent claims of the Gospel or identify it with Marxism must ponder these words:

> If the Church makes herself present in defence of, or in the advancement of, man she does so in line with her mission, which is religious and not social or political, and cannot fail to consider man in the entirety of his being . . . She does not need to have recourse to ideological systems in order to love, defend and collaborate in the liberation of man.

Having drawn attention to the "growing wealth of the few side by side with the growing poverty of the masses" the Pope went on to say:

> Those who bear responsibility for the public life of states and nations will have to understand that internal peace and international peace can only be ensured if a social and economic system based on justice flourishes.

The Papal tour of Latin America was undertaken in an atmosphere of encouragement to the weak, the oppressed, the under-privileged, the majority reduced to silence.

A very different aspect of the contemporary crisis in the Church centres round the name of Archbishop Marcel Lefebvre. The reader who has been dependent on certain English Catholic publications must be considerably bemused by the career of this very remarkable man, a man of exquisite courtesy, handsome, self-disciplined, pious. Why did one who served the African missionary Church so splendidly for thirty years, first in Gabon and then in Dakar where he handed over a highly organised Christian community to the African-born bishop whom he had himself led to the priesthood, where amid so many demanding tasks he also acted as Papal Delegate to all the French dependencies on the continent and Madagascar, why did this man who was further honoured by promotion to a European bishopric and then to the highest office in his own religious congregation turn after the Council to found a society of priests dedicated to disregard of much publicised conciliar ideas

and post-conciliar rules and regulations? Why did he count
on a certain following — as the present writer knows with
direct evidence that he did — and why is he, with the exception of Mother Teresa of Calcutta, the only religious leader
within the Catholic body who in the 1970s has been opening new houses? Most religious institutes and many dioceses
are selling off the ones they have.

Mgr Lefebvre was dismissed as a nuisance by those who
saw the Council as a triumph for their ideas, who remembered the strongly conservative part he played in the different sessions, who knew of his family background, which,
with snide allusions to the *Action Francaise* they presented
as old French, upper middle-class, diehard.* He was also a
figure to mock for who would heed him? That complacent
bubble was soon pricked. Events in his seminary at Ecône in
the Swiss canton of the Valais started, in the month of
June 1976, a series of shocks which rocked the French
Church. Mgr Lefebvre, against every plea and threat, ordained thirteen young priests and was suspended from
his priestly functions. He defied the penalty and celebrated
a public Mass in his native town of Lille on 29 August.

The Mass was attended by a crowd estimated between
5,000 and 10,000. This was the first news to the outside
world that a considerable section of French Catholics followed the Archbishop. The French Church had known this
already. What has been called the most sensational public
opinion poll in French religious history revealed that, even
after the suspension, twenty-eight per cent of those ques-
tioned supported the French prelate and only twenty-
three per cent disapproved of his conduct — the others
were undecided or non-committal.

If a thing is worth doing in France it is worth writing
about. Innumerable essays, articles, letters, reports appeared
in reviews and papers of every quality, allegiance, policy,
audience, on the Lefebvre question. More books were written about him than about any Catholic in recent times with

---

*He was never a member of the association.

the possible exception of John XXIII and John Paul II. The Catholic Right has lived with a feeling of dereliction since the Council. Not in France, where writers of the Right cover a vast spectrum and throw up every now and then brilliant stylists prepared to strike any opposing head in sight, even if there is a mitre on it. Who in the self-assured English Catholic press ever even mentions Fr R. L. Bruckberger, O.P., Michel de St Pierre, Michel Droit, Louis Salleron? The last three were, with others including the venerable Gustave Thibon, signatories to the letter asking Paul VI to lift the suspension on Archbishop Lefebvre.

Paul VI suffered bitterly from the evolving crisis. One of the Archbishop's grievances was the abolition of the so-called Tridentine Mass by the Pope. Paul wrote him five letters urging that he return to full obedience. The Pope had approved the ban on the seminary of Ecône, the condemnation of the French prelate by the Commission of Cardinals set up to investigate his case, and the final penalty, but influenced possibly by the volume of support and clutching at a final hope of reconciliation he gave the suspended cleric a special audience in the Vatican on 11 September 1976. Little came of it and the doctrinal position hardened, while recruits to Ecône continued to increase in number.

Paul VI possibly regretted the abrupt ending of the Tridentine Mass. He was challenged in his office as Pope by the principal theological manifesto published by Mgr Lefebvre, a document which appealed to tradition against certain theses and practices adopted since the Council.

We adhere with all our heart and with all our soul to Catholic Rome, the guardian of the Catholic Faith and to eternal Rome, mistress of wisdom and truth. On the other hand we refuse and have always refused to follow the Rome of the neo-modernist and neo-Protestant trend clearly manifested throughout Vatican II and, later, in all the reforms born of it. All these reforms have contributed and are still contributing to the destruction of the Church, the ruin of the Priesthood, the annihilation of the Sacrifice of the Mass and of the Sacraments, the disappearance of religious life, to naturalist, Teilhardian teaching in the universities, seminaries and catechesis, teaching born of liberalism and Protestantism many times condemned by the solemn teaching authority of the Church.

Mgr Lefebvre went on to declare that no one could oblige him and his supporters to abandon their faith, and he further developed his main criticism. True, Paul VI himself had denounced the tendency to "auto-destruction" within the Church.

On such views many who recognise the Archbishop's sincerity, courage and ability must part company with him. He takes his stand on tradition but tradition includes Vatican II rightly known. Yet his movement grows with some twenty houses in half-a-dozen countries, over eighty priests and 150 seminarists. It grows because in some regions, in France unfortunately, the reforms introduced since the Council have led to liturgical anarchy and doctrinal perversity: for France the evidence is in Michel de St Pierre's books, *Les Fumées de Satan* and *Le Ver est dans le fruit,* evidence gathered by André Mingot. The French bishops have, since the crucial year 1976, taken firm measures to remedy the disorders. The phrase "liturgical anarchy" was used by Dom Nau of Solesmes in a book defending the Mass of Paul VI.

The advent of a new Pope stirred hope of a break in the deadlock between Rome and Archbishop Lefebvre. John Paul II must, as he studied the relevant file, have seen the risk of reopening the matter. Would it not be better to leave it alone and not meet a setback if not outright failure? On the other hand there is a great deal at stake, not merely the future of the young priests ordained by Mgr Lefebvre, who in their present status cannot be given work; there is the expansion within the Catholic body of a very strong minority with the danger of eventual rupture.

Within five weeks of the Pope's election he met Mgr Lefebvre in a long audience. That was on 18 November 1978. The second stage in the negotiations, which many hope will be successful, began on 10 January 1979 when the French prelate went to see Cardinal Seper, Prefect of the Congregation of the Doctrine of the Faith — incidentally, in the Pope and Cardinal Seper the Archbishop was dealing with two men who represent areas where the Church has recently suffered persecution. An irony of the times was that previously he had been dealing with Frenchmen in Rome, Cardinals Villot and Garrone, the latter his former classmate at the Gregorian University.

John Paul II has left no doubt about his own theology of the Church and the Papacy. It was set forth fully in his first address to the College of Cardinals and in his first Encyclical, *Redemptor Hominis,* which was written in Polish and issued to the world on 11 March 1979.

Key passages in the address to the Cardinals are:

> We, therefore, consider it our primary duty to promote, with prudent but at the same time encouraging action, the most exact execution of the norms and directives of the Council, fostering above all the development of a proper mentality . . . The mystery of salvation which has its centre in the Church and is realised through it; the dynamism which in virtue of the same mystery animates the people of God; the special bond of collegiality which *cum Petro et sub Petro* binds the bishops together — all these elements on which we can never reflect enough, in our efforts to discover, in the light of human needs, both eternal and contingent, what modes of presence and courses of action the Church should adopt . . . We recommend in particular deeper reflection on the implications of collegiality, so that our minds might be better informed and that we might undertake our responsibilities more conscientiously . . . Called to the supreme responsibility in the Church, and placed in a position which obliges us to set an example of willing and doing, we, above all, must express this fidelity with all our strength, keeping intact the deposit of faith and fulfilling the special mandate of Christ, who, giving Simon the keys of the kingdom of heaven made him the "rock" on which he built the Church and commanded him to strengthen his brothers and to feed the sheep and lambs of his flock as a witness of love.

The Encyclical sets out to proclaim the Christian message in understandable modern idiom, to reassure Catholics confused by strident voices of dissent from within the Church, sometimes from its intelligentsia, to discern and judge, in the light of the Gospel, the grievous dangers to all men at the present time. The fundamental position taken in the Encyclical is the divine and fully human aspect of Redemption.

The Pope tells theologians what they ought not to do:

> Every theologian must be particularly aware of what Christ himself stated when he said: "The word which you hear is not mine but the Father's who sent me" (Jn 14:24). Nobody, therefore, can make of theology, as it were a simple collection of his own personal ideas, but everybody must be aware of being in close union with the mission of teaching truth for which the Church is responsible.

Those treating the Mass as a kind of high-minded togetherness must heed these words:

> When celebrating the Sacrament of the Body and Blood of the Lord, the full magnitude of the divine mystery must be respected, as must the full meaning of the sacramental sign in which Christ is really present and is received, the soul is filled with grace and the pledge of future glory is given.

The liturgical mavericks already referred to should read the Pope's words asking that "liturgical rules will be rigorously carried out". The splendid concluding section of John Paul II's Encyclical, which deals with Our Lady, is ready-made for the anthologies.

The passage in *Redemptor Hominis* on human rights and religious liberty has been much quoted and admired. There is realism, too, in the words on relief schemes to the developing nations, the Pope's application to our time of Christ's words to the blessed at the end of time: "I was hungry and you gave me to eat."

> These words become charged with even stronger warning, when we think that, instead of bread and cultural aid, the new states and nations awakening to indepen-

dent life are being offered, sometimes in abundance,
modern weapons and means of destruction placed at
the service of armed conflicts and wars that are not so
much a requirement for defending their just rights and
their sovereignty, but rather a form of chauvinism, im-
perialism and neocolonialism of one kind or another. We
all know well that the areas of misery and hunger on our
globe could have been made fertile in a short time if the
gigantic investments for armaments at the service of war
and destruction had been changed into investments for
food at the service of life.

Strong words, echoing Paul VI's appeal at the Eucharistic
Congress in Bombay for a similar change of heart and deed.
John Paul II will be forgiven, in his preoccupation with the
nations of the world, for an occasional thought of his own
homeland. Due, it is said, to the influence of Gierek, the
attitude of the civil authorities was, at the time of the
election, correct and respectful. A large delegation was
present at the Enthronement Mass. The papal visit to Poland,
which many hoped would take place in May for the ninth
centenary of St Stanislaus, has been fixed for June. The
Pope himself inaugurated on Sunday, 8 January, the
weekly Mass in Polish broadcast from Vatican Radio. Cardinal Wyszynski, in his first sermon in Warsaw after the
papal election, asked again that Mass for the sick and aged
be allowed on Polish Radio. He also asked for the ending
of censorship, adding characteristically for a Pole, that "if
the censors were put on pension, the taxpayers would not
object".

8   Homecoming

John Paul II's visit to Poland seized the imagination of the world with an impact even greater than his election had done. For nine full days he and the Polish people together enacted a series of astonishing episodes immense in scale and replete with Christian meaning, each of which was watched by millions thanks to television. It was a succession of real life tableaux which seemed spread out before the viewer by a mighty miraculous hand.

The moment in the new pontificate was right for such an event. The preliminaries were over. The new Pope had taken the reins of government firmly in hand; he had accomplished the essential duties of his office and presided over great characteristic ceremonies of the Papacy. In the area of universal Church government he was determined to maintain the enlarged College of Cardinals established by Paul VI and had appointed fifteen new members.

Before leaving Rome early on the morning of Saturday, 2 June, John Paul II spoke briefly but movingly to the civil authorities come to bid him farewell. He was leaving the country of his choice for the country of his origin, the Pope said. He outlined the itinerary he would follow, paid tribute to the Polish hierarchy and its head, Cardinal Wyszynski, and had a very generous word of gratitude for the President of the Polish Council of State, Henryk Jablonski: "I renew herewith my most sincere appreciation to the authority of the Polish state confirming what I have already expressed in my letter: my attachment to the cause of peace, of co-existence and of cooperation between nations; the hope that my visit will strengthen internal unity between my beloved fellow-countrymen and will also serve the eventual development of relations between State and Church." In the same spirit the travelling Pope sent conventional but warmly phrased telegrams of greetings to the heads of the states which he flew over on his way to Warsaw.

Bells rang joyously throughout his homeland as the Boeing 727, Citta di Bergamo, of Alitalia Airline, piloted by the fleet commander, began its descent to Okecie military airport near Warsaw. After the touchdown Cardinal Wyszynski entered the plane and personally welcomed the Pope. Then John Paul II descended, knelt and kissed the ground of his native land. Formal greetings were offered on behalf of the government and the nation by President Jablonski, on behalf of the "Catholic Church, the episcopate, the clergy and the people of God" by the Primate. In the first address of the visit the Pope emphasised the strictly religious motive of his journey; he added that he hoped, too, that benefits of the kind he had mentioned at Rome airport would accrue from it.

Then followed the triumphal entry to Warsaw, the first contact with the throngs of delighted Polish citizens, the crowds that were through the week to surge everywhere in such numbers and impress foreigners by their orderly behaviour, their deep recollection in moments of prayer, their unashamed piety. The procession reached the Cathedral, where the strictly religious ceremony, the meeting between the Pope and the diocesan authorities, took place.

John Paul's opening words were a hymn of praise of the Cardinal Primate and he had words of affectionate fellowship, too, for the other dignitaries. The former Archbishop of Krakow recalled that Warsaw's cathedral had shared the city's fate, but has risen from the ashes.

Before the multitude massed on Victory Square a little later for the first open-air Mass the theme of martyred Warsaw was more explicit. It was taken up first by the Cardinal in his address of welcome. The Pope, for his part, spoke of the context of his visit, the wish of Paul VI, which through him was being fulfilled, to come as a pilgrim to Poland; he reminded his listeners of the Millennium of Poland's faith and the ninth centenary of St Stanislaus

which he was honouring. Looking almost in a detached way
at the special witness which Poland was, in our time, called
to give, he held aloft the explanation of its mysterious
survival: Christ, who cannot be excluded from the story
of man. He spoke of the witness of Warsaw itself and
coupled with his tribute to the heroic city words of praise
for the unknown soldier — with whom he identified all
those who spend themselves in the service of the country.

It was on the level of patriotism also that he met the
party leaders on the same day. Gierek kept to the line which
he had followed in his meeting with Paul VI: emphasis on
the contribution of the Holy See to détente and disarma-
ment; he added a word not so often heard from his col-
leagues, recognition of the Church's role in the struggle
against the Nazis. Church and State were, he thought, working together.

John Paul II's reply will be closely analysed by students
of Church-State relations; it continued logically the theme
expressed earlier in this book. He referred to the encounter
between Gierek and Paul VI and enunciated a number of
principles which would justify optimism in this whole area.
The Church, as Polish history exemplifies, strengthens man
in his natural social bonds.

> This comes from the fundamental mission of the Church
> which is ambitious above all to make man better, more
> conscious of his dignity, more devoted in life to his
> domestic, social, professional and patriotic duties: to
> render man more confident, more courageous, conscious
> of his rights and duties, socially responsible, creative and
> useful. For this activity the Church does not want privi-
> leges, but only and exclusively what is indispensable to
> the accomplishment of its mission.

The Pope, as his predecessor had done, singled out for com-
mendation the positive achievements of the regime.

That initial basic statement of coexistence informed all
that was to follow; it should be borne in mind when reading
comments that the government was perturbed by John
Paul's later references to human rights, by his alleged entry

to the closed domain of politics. There is little hard evidence for any such apprehension by the rulers, whatever some lesser party members may have felt. There was no doubt what the feelings were of his audience at the Mass before St Anne's church on Pentecost Sunday for the university students: little doubt that his words will be treasured by them and all those in like position. This was a world which he knew intimately, its idiom and outlook familiar to him through years of experience.

A new phase of the papal pilgrimage began on the same day in the ancient primatial city of Gniesno. The Pope arrived by helicopter to find an immense crowd awaiting him. Formal greetings were pronounced again by the Cardinal Primate, this time with a strong touch of local colour and local history, the history made by the saints of Gniesno.

The papal reply centred on catechesis, for on this spot, as he said, was begun the catechetical instruction of the Polish people. The remarks appeared harmless but they bore on a matter of crucial importance in the country at the present time, the provision of adequate religious instruction. As if to keep the subject in low key, and at the same time to do some instructing himself, the Pope gave free rein to his audience on each occasion that he met them — to sing hymns, exchange compliments, even witticisms. Indeed, eventually, as evening wore on and the enraptured crowd showed no sign of fatigue, no wish to part company with their idol, Cardinal Wyszynski had, more than once, to plead with the Pope, which only drew another sally from one who was enjoying himself immensely: "I'm in trouble with the Cardinal."

But the written word remains. There may have been interruptions, there may have been off the cuff additions to the texts. They remain, and remain impressive, by their intellectual substance. At the Mass before the cathedral the Pope spoke of the spiritual unity of Christian Europe; to the young people he spoke of the Christian inspiration of Polish culture.

The atmosphere and theme of the feast they were celebrating that day, Pentecost, influenced the Pope's words, the flow of this thought. The pentecostal theme was not absent from his talk on Polish culture to his young audience. He reminded them that the earliest literary document known in their country was the famous *Bogurodzica* (Mother of God), attributed by tradition to St Adalbert but certainly medieval in origin: it is a combination of hymn — always sung with sentiments of reverence — and profession of faith. "Polish culture", the Pope could say, "since its very beginnings bears very clear Christian marks."

The following day, Whit Monday, he was at the heart of Catholic Poland, Czestochowa. Before leaving Gniesno early in the morning he met the diocesan seminarists — he was to have met them the evening before but the crowd of youthful enthusiasts massed before the cathedral had, with his happy complicity, upset his schedule. Landing by helicopter at Czestochowa the Pope had, besides the official reception, a greeting that must have gone straight to his heart: a hundred little boys and girls in first communion dress ran forward to meet him and each of them offered him a flower.

John Paul II listened to the Primate tell briefly of the mighty things accomplished by God through the intervention of Our Lady of Czestochowa: the Cardinal recalled the crisis of the Millennium period, the measures taken by the hierarchy, the programme of national renewal in the religious, moral and social domains linked with the novena of preparation for the Millennium, the Marian initiative of the Polish bishops at the Council. The Pope, he said, was celebrating the feast of Mary, Mother of the Church, which Paul VI had conceded to the dioceses of Poland; the feast fell on that very day, 4 June.

John Paul went into the recent history of the shrine and then widened his perspective to take in great principles of Marian doctrine and important practices of devotion to Our Lady:

> All things through Mary. This is the authentic interpretation of the presence of the Mother of God in the mystery of Christ and of the Church, as chapter VIII of the

Constitution *Lumen Gentium* proclaims it. Such an interpretation matches the tradition of the Saints, Bernard
of Clairvaux, Grignion de Montfort, Maximilian Kolbe.

He renewed the act of consecration to Mary made by
the Polish bishops on 3 May 1966 and approved in a special
Bull by Paul VI.

> Today his unworthy successor coming to Jasna Gora
> wishes to renew this act on the day following Pentecost,
> they day on which throughout all Poland the feast of
> the Mother of the Church is celebrated. For the first
> time the Pope celebrates this solemnity and along with
> you, venerable and dearest brothers, expresses gratitude
> to his great predecessor who from the days of the Coun-
> cil began to invoke Mary by the title Mother of the
> Church.

One immediate result of the act of consecration must
have been an increase in the physical and psychic energy of
the Pope himself. Romans have been awestruck by the heavy
schedule he fulfills day after day. From now on in Poland
he surpassed himself with a programme of religious ceremonies and talking engagements which would have provided adequate work for three other men.

In the afternoon of the first day at Czestochowa he went
to the parish church of St Sigismund, which is near the
monastery. The parish was awaiting the visit of the Madonna
of Jasna Gora, that is of the copy of the icon blessed, as
John Paul II recalled, by Pius XII in 1957. The idea was
that it should be borne from one city to another throughout
the whole country. As Cardinal Wojtyla he had welcomed
the icon, he reminded his audience, in Krakow. He dwelt on
the significance of this practice and again expounded the
meaning of the Marian cult and of its fruitfulness in Poland.
The reader should remember what has been said in a former
chapter on the meaning of the icon in the Christian orient.

Next morning, at 7.30, the Pope met the Polish nuns.
They were assembled before the open-air altar on the espla-
nade in thousands. In the homily of the Mass they heard
words of encouragement made convincing by an informed

insight into their vocation. The Pope repeated to them what
he had said to his first audience of nuns, the 20,000 who
assembled in Rome soon after his election, what he had
said to the superiors general of religious, what he had said to
the nuns he met in Mexico. Pointing to the Virgin of the
Annunciation as their model he continued:

> In these words is contained, in a certain way, the pro-
> totype of every religious profession through which each
> of you embraces with her whole being the mystery of
> grace contained in the religious vocation. Each of you,
> like Mary, chooses Jesus the divine Spouse. The living
> sign which each of you embodies in the midst of men is
> inestimable. Embracing the divine Spouse with faith,
> hope and charity you embrace him in the countless
> people you serve, in the sick, the aged, the maimed, the
> handicapped, those with whom none but you can deal
> because it demands a truly heroic spirit of sacrifice.

That is John Paul II at his best: the high ideal and the sense
of human need, compassion for the human condition.

At ten o'clock that day, in the ancient library of the
Paulite monastery, the Pope met the national episcopal conference in their one hundred and sixty-ninth session. His
address to this assembly was the longest and most thought-
ful which he made during his visit, and detailed quotation
from it or analysis of its contents will belong to a larger
study than this. Its contents will help to continue the reflections set down earlier on the evolving relations between
Church and State in Poland. The Pope sketched with broad,
suggestive strokes the story of such relations in past times,
mentioning St Adalbert, delaying on St Stanislaus, whose
name from now on enters the papal pilgrimage rather explicitly. He referred, too, to the vexed question of the
western and northern provinces – the territories formerly
occupied by Germany – happily solved by Paul VI.

John Paul's chief interest, however, was in the achieve-
ment of normal relations between Church and State at the
present time. A basic directive in this undertaking would be
the text of Vatican II on Religious Liberty. The Pope

quoted from his address to the diplomatic corps on 12 January, one passage of which will bear repetition here:

> The Apostolic See is always ready, as it has already shown, to manifest its openness towards every country or regime, seeking the essential good which is the authentic good of man. A certain number of demands correlative to this good have been expressed in the "Declaration of the Rights of Man" and in international treaties which give it concrete application.

The Pope then broached the delicate question of dialogue between Church and State in Poland:

> The Polish episcopate has its own particular experience in this important domain. Proceeding from the documents of Vatican II, it has produced a theoretical ensemble of documents known to the Apostolic See and, at the same time, has drawn up an ensemble of practical pastoral attitudes which demonstrate readiness for dialogue. These texts show clearly that authentic dialogue must respect the convictions of believers, and secure all the citizens' rights, and normal conditions for the activity of the Church as a religious community to which the very great majority of Poles belong. We recognise that this dialogue cannot be easy since it proceeds from conceptions of the world diametrically opposed, but it must be possible if the good of man and the nation demands it.

Principles should be in all areas quite clear, the Pope thought, and normal relations would be helped by the current insistence on human rights, which include the right to religious liberty.

The Pope briefly addressed the episcopal commission on science and he also gave a short sermon on the Angelus in the Roman manner, urging fidelity to the devotion. Upwards of a million Silesians had come to Czestochowa on the same day and to them, the Pope, conscious of their proximity to the new western frontier, conscious too of past disputes, which he gracefully covered with the phrase "the long story of human vicissitudes and works of divine

Providence", now proposed as a model and intercessor the noble figure of St Hedwig, equally venerated by Poles and Germans. He reminded his listeners that he had been elected Pope on her feastday, 16 October, and charged them to present his prayer at her shrine in Trzebnica. Then he held up the ideal of national unity and of reconciliation between peoples, extolling the family as the true foundation of national greatness.

The papal pilgrim may appear spendthrift of his time and energy when it is noted that on this crowded day he still would be present at the devotions which every evening take place at nine o'clock and would still preach to those present, avid for his words of faith and hope and love. Next day he was equally prodigal of his eloquence. At seven o'clock the papal suite assembled in the chapel of the icon to assist at the papal Mass and hear the Holy Father consecrate all his close helpers to Our Lady of Czestochowa. An hour later, seminarists, so numerous in this Catholic land, saw and admired a former Polish seminarist, one whose life span was not so remote from theirs, clothed in the white robes of the papacy. His seminary days had been precarious and perilous. He made no reference to such things. The burden of his discourse was the new life in Christ.

> This new life which Christ gives us has become our spiritual life, our interior life. Let us accordingly discover ourselves; let us discover in ourselves the interior man with his quality, talents, noble desires, ideals, but let us discover, too, the weaknesses, the vices, wicked inclinations: egoism, pride, sensuality. Let us realise perfectly how the first aspects of our nature deserve to be developed and strengthened, how much, on the contrary, the second must be overcome, resisted, transformed.

After the seminarists, future priests, came those already on the ministry. John Paul II went to the cathedral of the Holy Family to meet the secular and religious priests of the diocese of Czestochowa. Introducing him, the bishop, Dr Barela, began: "I salute the Polish priest who has mounted the throne of Peter." The Pope quoted to them what he had said on the occasion of his first meeting with the diocesan and religious priests of Rome, what he had said to the priests of Mexico in the sanctuary of Our Lady of Guadalupe, what he had written in his letter to the priests of the world. The third quotation summed up the outlook, and, in many ways, the conduct of the man himself: "Our pastoral activity demands that we should be close to men and to all their problems whether personal, domestic or social, but it still demands that we be close to these problems as priests. Only then, within the limits of all these problems, do we remain ourselves."

It has been well said that he who can sanctify the priests of the Church will sanctify the whole Church and save the world. John Paul II has, in the short time of his pontificate, shown that he realises this very fully: "Let us reflect with humility", he said to his fellow priests,

> on the confidence which the Master and Redeemer has in us, entrusting to our priestly hand the power over his Body and his Blood. I want to hope that in these difficult times you will be able so to bear yourselves that "your light will shine before men". Let us pray incessantly for this. Let us pray for it with great humility. Love Mary, dear brothers. From this love do not cease to draw strength for your hearts. She shows herself for you and through you the Mother of all, who thirst so much for this motherhood: *Monstra te esse matrem, sumat par te preces, qui pro nobis natus, tulit esse tuus.*

At a quarter past two in the afternoon of this fifth day, more than six thousand professors, students, past pupils and friends from the University of Lublin were crowded into the main Basilica of the monastery, awaiting the Pope and praying. He came among them to touch off scenes of great joy and enthusiasm. There was an official address of welcome, a procession of gifts, words from the Pope, who was constantly interrupted as elsewhere by applause and by songs in which he joined — a running dialogue exuberant, respectful and gay — and to wind it all up the old European university song, *Guadeamus igitur juvenes dum sumus.*

The Pope spoke to them for half an hour and then went to say Mass for the multitude of workers from Upper Silesia and the miners of Zaglebie, the latter in dress uniform, head plumes and all. This is the population of the industrial heart of Poland, whose practice of the Catholic faith is, viewing their circumstances and their working conditions, unique in the world. These are the men who assemble in hundreds of thousands annually on the feastday (on the feastday only men are allowed entry) at the shrine of Our Lady of Piekary: in 1978 Cardinal Wojtyla had addressed them.

Bishop Herbert Bednorz of Katowice reminded the Pope of these things in his formal address, as he also spoke of the difficulties the workers had experienced in coming to see the Pope. There had been work as usual and some had already a night's work done when they set out by makeshift transport of different kinds for Czestochowa.

So the miners sang their hearts out as the Pope appeared: their hymn, "Let us sing to the Queen of the Angels". He spoke to them of the essential meaning of work: "Work should help man to better himself, become spiritually more mature, more responsible so that he may be able to realise his vocation on earth whether as an irreproducible person, whether in community with others, above all in the fundamental human community, the family." John Paul, the former quarry worker, urged the Silesian workers to remain true to God:

> Dearest brothers and sisters, you men who have hard work in Silesia, Zaglebie and in all Poland! Do not allow yourselves to be seduced by the temptation that man can fulfil himself by denying God, eliminating prayer from life, existing only as a worker, deluding himself with the idea that his products can meet the needs of the human heart.

If the workers began with a hymn to Our Lady, the Pope ended with a prayer to her. In the evening before leaving Czestochowa he spoke once again, words of farewell, words of intense fervour directed to Our Lady, renewing in detail his act of universal consecration, concluding: "To you I consecrate Rome and Poland united through your servant by a new bond of love."

That evening the former archbishop of Krakow was back in the city which had meant so much in his life. On arrival he spoke on this theme, then went to his former cathedral on the Wawel to offer his benediction to the priestly body he had known so well and to all the People of God. No one was omitted from the roll-call of remembrance and love which he read out. He had thus completed his seventh speaking engagement of the day. His remarks were relevant to each audience, with nothing banal, little, practically no, platitude. His amazing personality made its impact constantly. For the last days of his visit, spent in and around Krakow, the crowds rose to their peak in numbers, in enthusiasm and in prayer. With this crescendo one feels the presence of a phenomenon unique in world history. A million people crowded into Krakow on the first night of splendour; at Auschwitz next day and out in the foothills of the Tatra mountains at Nowy Targ two days later, estimates go to three quarters of a million and for the final Mass in Krakow "meadow" on Sunday, *L'Osservatore Romano* mentions three million, the equivalent of the entire population of the Republic of Ireland. Those who watched the ceremonies on television know that the masses of human beings stretched away to the horizon.

The Poles in the worst days of Stalinism discovered a law which worked to their advantage: you cannot put the whole town in jail. Now it was the witness of the whole nation. What can anyone do against that? Not that the regime wished to create any serious handicap to the manifestations of piety and papal sentiment. One or two excited commentators seemed to want some kind of clash, at least confrontation, and hoped that the vast numbers in Krakow would be the background. The same people thought, apparently, that the Pope was talking politics and that the government was both surprised and annoyed.

John Paul II was, in his references to the world of politics, circumspect, wise and, in fact, restrained. With the whole

Polish hierarchy before him he could have referred to the detention of the Cardinal in Stalinist times. He could have spoken of the imprisonment of bishops, the sham trials of the Bishop of Kielce, Dr Kaczmarek, singled out for especially harsh treatment, of the vindictive measures inflicted on the former Administrator of Krakow, Eugenius Baziak and his Vicar General, Bishop Stanislas Rospond, both driven from the diocese; and a still more pointed occasion was given him by the presence of the Bishop of Katowice, Dr Bednorz, the victim of similar meaningless expulsion.

Nor did the pilgrim Pope dwell on the petty harrassment which still continues in various sectors of Catholic life. In the two speeches which dealt most explicitly with Church-State relations the note was primarily constructive and optimistic. The reference to human rights, in particular the right to religious liberty, was made with a view to the continuation and improvement of the present position. The image of a thoughtless crusader scattering quotes of an explosive kind is an invention of a few journalists hungry for the unusual and sensational. The Pope certainly extemporised in the course of his speeches, but not in those mentioned and not, so far as reliable information goes, in any way that essentially differed from the content of the speeches integrally reproduced in *L'Osservatore Romano*.

It was, then, in a spirit of peace and reconciliation that the Bishop of Rome exercised his pastoral ministry in the diocese of Krakow from which he had been called to the See of Peter. These three days were filled with reminiscence, nostalgia, gratitude, piety and witness to the highest human and Christian values. The piety was dominant in the visit on 7 June to Kalvaria Zebrzydowska, a place beloved of the Pope in his Krakow days. He told the story of the crowning of the image of the Madonna in the central Basilica — there are many chapels and oratories to evoke the incidents of the Passion — by Cardinal Albino Dunajewski, with a diadem offered by Leo XIII, on 15 August 1887. Again he abounded in reflections on the role of Mary, Mother of God. He urged the faithful to continue to visit the sanctuary, to pray there — "this simple and fundamental invitation of the Pope to prayer: it is the most important invitation; it is the most essential message".

Reminiscence and nostalgia characterised the visit on the same day to the birthplace of John Paul II, Wadowice. He was happy, he said, to meet the inhabitants of the town, but he thought of the earlier generation, those who had seen the inter-war period. There was, of course, a special word for the parish priest, Mgr Zacher, the former teacher of Karol Wojtyla. The Pope went to the church of his baptism and kissed the font at which he had been given the sacrament. He saw again the church of the Carmelites, founded by a venerable Servant of God towards the end of the last century, scene of his first contact with the Order of St John of the Cross, whose writings he would study, whose religious habit he thought for a while of taking.

It is a far cry from the contemplative heights of Carmelite spirituality to the infamy of twentieth-century mass-murder. In the afternoon of that day John Paul II went to Auschwitz-Birkenau; appropriately the same day that he had so vividly relived the events of the Passion and death of Christ at Kalvaria Zebrzydowska.

When this place of infamy was being shown on the television and cinema screens of the world in the film *Holocaust*, did anyone for a moment imagine that a Pope would go to pray there, to appeal from the scene of the massacre to the sanity of mankind to end the possibility of such horror. The personal link was Blessed Maximilian Kolbe, Karol Wojtyla's hero. He knelt there on the spot where the Franciscan died. He went to pray at the Wall of Death. Then surrounded by a vast throng he led a concelebrated Mass. Those who saw it on their television screens will have seen the streamer in the stripes of the Auschwitz internees with Maximilian Kolbe's convict number inscribed on it. There was, they will remember, something more poignant. The concelebrating priests were former inmates of concentration camps. But the offertory procession was led by three former inmates of Auschwitz, dressed in striped uniforms of the

same meagre kind that they were condemned to wear in
jail. Later they were presented to the Holy Father with their
relatives. He met the man for whom Maximilian Kolbe had
died, who had also been present in St Peter's in Rome when
the Franciscan was beatified.

Certain events are themselves testimony more eloquent
than any words. A Pope at Auschwitz to say Mass is in itself
such an event. But for those who would not look at things
with the eyes of faith there was a homily in which the lesson
sealed with four million lives was simply but unforgettably
stated. The two heroic figures of Auschwitz enabled the
speaker to lead his listeners to the heart of its strange mystery: Kolbe and Edith Stein.

These had died on a spot where "the dignity of man had
been trampled on in horrendous fashion", where "victory
had been won by faith and love."

> Is it then to be wondered at in any way that the Pope
> who was born and educated in this land, the Pope who
> came to the See of Peter from the diocese wherein Ausch-
> witz camp stands, has begun his first Encyclical with the
> words *Redemptor hominis* and has devoted it altogether
> to the cause of man, to the dignity of man, to the threats
> against him and finally to his inalienable rights which so
> easily can be trampled on and annihilated by his fellows?
> Is it not enough to clothe a man in a different uniform,
> to equip him with the apparatus of violence, to impose
> on him an ideology in which the rights of man are sub-
> ordinate to the demands of the system, completely sub-
> ordinate, for such things to become fact?

The Pope said that he had often come to Auschwitz in
former times, to "this Golgotha of the contemporary world",
to these tombs, mostly nameless. "I could not *not come* as
Pope". He named some of the commemorative tablets.

> In particular I linger with you, dear participants in this
> encounter, before the stone which bears a Hebrew in-
> scription. This inscription evokes the memory of the
> people whose sons and daughters were destined to total
> extermination. This people has its origin in Abraham,
> who is the father of our faith (cf.Rom 4:12), as Paul of

Tarsus put it. This people who especially had received from God the commandment "Thou shalt not kill" had experienced in a particular way in itself what it means to be killed. Before this stone no one ought to pass by indifferently.

Recalling the Russian inscription, the Pope said he would refrain from comment. He paid tribute to the "part played by this nation in the last terrible war for the liberation of peoples".

The lesson? That proclaimed by Paul VI at the United Nations — no more war — recognition, as John XXIII sought, of the dignity of the human person, assurance of the rights of nations, finally the concept of love in its most comprehensive meaning:

This commandment takes concrete form in the respect of others, of their personality, of their conscience, it takes concrete form in "dialogue with others", in knowing how to seek out and recognise what may be good and positive in those who have different ideas from us, in those too who, in good faith, are sincerely in error.

In condemning servitude, conquest, outrage, exploitation, murder, the Pope added to the voice of John XXIII and Paul VI that of "the son of a nation which has in its ancient and recent history suffered from others manifold torment. I do not say it by way of accusation but for remembrance." The Pope had earlier said that the millionfold murder of his fellow countrymen was another "sorrowful reckoning for the conscience of mankind".

Nowy Targ was a change from this sombre canvas. As Cardinal Wojtyla had often gone to Auschwitz to pray and meditate on the human condition, so he had gone to the Tatra mountains for relaxation and to commune with nature. The region of Podhale rose to his visit. How many crossed the nearby frontier of Czechoslovakia is not known; there was a wish from the neighbouring countries, from their rulers, that television transmitters in the border regions would be turned down. The hundreds of thousands who had converged on the provisional wooden chapel were free from worry of any kind, whether about regimes or not.

They did not need a spokesman. But Archbishop Macharski, successor to the Pope in the See of Krakow and cardinal-designate, felt it his duty to welcome the distinguished visitor: "You loved this land, which is perhaps the most beautiful border region of Poland. You loved the people who dwell in this region."

Prelates from other countries had had the thought of coming to Poland during the papal visit and some were present at Nowy Targ. Archbishop Macharski spoke for all his fellow-countrymen when he said: "We are filled with joy at this encounter. We are happy to have with us so many guests, as witnesses. We offer our welcome to all."

The theme of the papal address was the right of man to work and to ownership of land.

> This is a great and fundamental right of man: the right to work and the right to land. Although the development of the economy carries us in another direction, although the provision of a base for industrialisation is to be valued, although the present-day generation is in large numbers leaving the countryside and work in the fields, none the less, the right to own land constitutes the basis of sound economy and sociology.

The personal link with the land had been always the strength of the Polish people.

The Pope had earlier spoken of the beauty of the Tatra district, of the repose which people sought there, as he himself knew by experience. Later, he urged the young people present to think of the spiritual refreshment which would be so salutary to them, which they would also find there. He commended them to the patroness of Podhale, Our Lady of Ludzmierz; he was celebrating Mass before her miraculous statue which had been brought by the faithful to the chapel erected for the papal ceremony.

In Krakow there were several important meetings to address. The speaker was able to change the key as the character of each audience needed. It was sheer fulfilment and a note of high ecclesiastical order and tradition at the

final session of the Synod of Krakow. This had been initiated
on 8 May 1972, timed to end 8 May 1979 with the ninth
centenary of St Stanislaus. John Paul II said simply that
when beginning the vast undertaking, which involved so
many commissions, he did not think that he would con-
clude it as a guest from Rome.

The Pope was asked not to visit the church of Nowa
Huta. He went then to the Cistercian monastery of Mogila
nearby. He spoke of the singular story of the Nowa Huta
church, pointing to its source of power: the Cross of Christ.
That evening the Pope met the numerous ecclesiastical
delegations come to Krakow to rejoice with him, to afford
moral support to the Polish Church. There were cardinals
and bishops from Europe, North and South America and
the Third World. Cardinal Gray of Scotland, Cardinal-
designate Ó Fiaich of Armagh and some Irish bishops were
among the number.

Next day was the fitting climax to the nine days visit.
Nothing was forgotten. The Pope spoke in several languages
to the journalists who had come to report on his visit. He
had a delicate word of thanks and congratulation for the
President of the Republic who came to see him off: "This
was an act of courage on both sides but one that was needed."
He left a more important souvenir to the one whose praise
he had chanted throughout his pilgrimage: he solemnly
crowned the Krakow Madonna of Makow. And before
the largest crowd ever assembled anywhere in the presence
of a Pope he delivered a stirring oration which gathered
together all the themes of the visit and recalled the great
moment of history they were celebrating; the martyrdom
of St Stanislaus. He urged the faithful of Krakow and of
Poland to stand firm, loyal to Christ and to their country,
indomitable. That evening he flew back to the Eternal City,
to an official welcome at the the airport, which he gracefully acknowledged, and to the acclamation of a hundred
thousand Romans and pilgrims in St Peter's Square.

Select Bibliography

This Bibliography lists mostly primary documentation.

Actes et Documents du Saint Siège relatifs à la seconde guerre mondiale, III, Le Saint Siège et la situation religieuse en Pologne et dans les pays baltes, 2 Vols, Rome, Vatican Press, 1967

Andrews, T. *The Polish National Catholic Church in America and Poland*, London, SPCK, 1953

Blit, L., *The Eastern Pretender*, London, 1965

Christian Social Association, *Information Bulletin*, monthly, Warsaw: accurate news and full reproduction of important texts and addresses

Congar, Y. M., *La crise dans l'Eglise et Mgr Lefebvre*, Paris, 1976; published in English as *Challenge to the Church*

Documentation Catholique, Paris: regular "dossiers" on Poland

Galter, A., *The Red Book of the Persecuted Church*, Dublin, 1957

Lapide, P., *The last three Popes and the Jews*, London, 1967

Lefebvre, M., *A Bishop Speaks*, Edinburgh, 1975

Martin, A., *La Pologne défend son âme*, Paris, 1977; invaluable documentation

Mindszenty, Jozef Cardinal, *Memoirs*, London, 1974

Szoldrski, O.W., C.SS.R., *Martyrologium Cleri Polonici sub occupatione Germanica, 1939-1945*, Rome, 1965: the official list.

Wyszynski, Stefan Cardinal, *Work*, London, 1966; *A Strong Man Armed*, sermons, London, 1966

Philosophical and theological works by John Paul II mentioned in the text are widely available in translation, as are his poems.